B. Tipton

Succeeding With Difficult Students™

Workbook

A Publication of Lee Canter & Associates

Staff Writer
Marcia Shank

Editorial Staff
Marlene Canter
Jacqui Hook
Patricia Sarka
Kathy Winberry

Design
Bob Winberry

©1993 Lee Canter & Associates
P.O. Box 2113, Santa Monica, CA 90407-2113
800-262-4347 310-395-3221

Printed in the United States of America
First printing April 1993

97 96 95   10 9 8 7 6 5 4

ISBN 0-939007-53-3

Contents

Succeeding With Difficult Students™

Introduction

Who are difficult students?

Difficult students are the students who are continually disruptive, persistently defiant, demanding of attention or unmotivated. They are the students who defy your authority and cause you stress, frustration and anger. Many of these students have severe emotional or behavioral problems. They may have been physically or psycho-logically abused, or born substance addicted to alcohol, crack or other drugs. Many of them come from home environments where parents have minimal, if any, influence or control over their behavior.

Difficult students are not the students in your class who act up occasionally. They're not the ones who once in awhile may cause you to lose your temper. Difficult students are those who engage in disruptive, off-task behavior with great intensity and frequency.

These are the students with whom your regular classroom management efforts do not work.

There is no question that difficult students present a greater challenge today than ever before. Teachers are frustrated because of the disruptions these students cause to the rest of the class, and also because they seem to defy all their best-intentioned efforts to reach them. With difficult students, a teacher often simply reacts to genuine feelings of frustration based on past experiences, and the student is quickly labeled.

Once a student is labeled (hyperactive, Attention Deficit Disorder, or just plain impossible), what are his or her chances of ever being seen as a unique individual with potential for succeeding at school? Once a student is labeled, it's all too easy to drop responsibility—to feel that the student has too many problems—that there's "nothing I can do."

When nothing seems to work with them, difficult students tend to make you forget the confidence you once had in your ability to positively impact each and every student.

You can turn this situation around.

You can help the difficult students in your own classroom have a positive school experience this year, raise their self-esteem and increase their self-confidence.

It starts with taking a look at your own perceptions.

Most students arrive in your classroom with a basic foundation of trust in school, and teachers in particular. Their parents have supported their efforts and have motivated them to behave and succeed in school. These students have had positive experi-ences with teachers and have received self-esteem building reinforcement and encouragement from both home and school.

Based on their past successful experi-ences, these students—the majority of your class—are able to trust you, and trust that what you ask of them is in their best inter-est. Because they are able to trust, they are able to accept your guidance.

The difficult student, on the other hand, comes to the classroom with a different perception based upon very different experiences. Many come from home environments where the parents themselves had negative school experiences, and where respect for teacher and school has not been communicated. Other students come from homes where the adults in their lives have been unreliable role models, unresponsive, abusive or simply overwhelmed and unable to meet their children's needs for motivation and support.

Whatever the origin, these students enter school with a deficit of trust in schools, and in the adults who are there to teach and guide them.

As they begin their school years, then, these students do not instinctively trust that what a teacher asks of them is in their best interest. When asked to do something, to cooperate, to become responsible members of the class, their responses are often negative and defiant. *"You can't make me!"* This hostility is both hurtful and anger-provoking to the teacher who starts off with the best of intentions toward the student. Consequently, the teacher's frustration grows and his or her confidence and self-esteem drop.

And what happens next? Continued defiant responses from the student tend to provoke defiant, negative responses from the teacher and a downward spiral is set into motion. The student's self-esteem is lowered, making his or her chances for success even dimmer. Trust is never established, and ultimately these students fulfill the expectations that seem to have been there for them from the start. They do not do well in school. School continues to be a negative experience.

Building trust is the first step toward succeeding with difficult students.

Working successfully with difficult students begins then with a major shift in attitude. Put yourself in your student's shoes. Look at the world from his eyes—from his past experiences. Recognize that with these students your expectations that "he should trust me, and listen to me   I only want the best for him" are not realistic. This is a trust that hasn't been there, but a trust that must be nurtured before the student can be motivated to behave and do well in school.

Building trust with a difficult student will be an ongoing process. You will need to take specific steps to establish a positive relationship with this student. You will have to develop behavior management techniques that recognize his or her individual needs. And you will have to communicate in a manner that is responsive and caring, yet firm.

As you proceed through this workbook, keep in mind that building trust is the foundation of everything you want to achieve with a difficult student. Through your words, and through your actions, communicate both your commitment, your concern and your confidence. Empower yourself to develop a relationship with this student that can literally turn his or her life around.

Helping difficult students will be among the greatest professional experiences of your career. You can have pride and confidence in knowing that you've done the best you can and that your students have benefited.

For a comprehensive understanding of Lee Canter's Succeeding With Difficult Students™ program, please read the *Succeeding With Difficult Students* text.

How to Use This Book

The *Succeeding With Difficult Students Workbook* will guide you through a step-by-step approach for individualizing your behavior management efforts with a difficult student. You will begin by identifying *why* a specific student misbehaves and then proceed to developing strategies you will use to help this student learn to behave more appropriately.

Follow these guidelines:

1 Read "Before You Begin" (page 7). This checklist of classroom behavior management considerations will help you focus on whether excessive disruptive behavior within your class is caused by a large number of difficult students or problems in overall behavior management.

   Teachers sometimes find that by focusing their efforts on classwide behavior management they decrease the disruptive behavior of some of their "difficult" students.

2 Identify your difficult student(s)—the ones you have determined simply will not respond to your regular behavior management efforts. Keep in mind that you are making a commitment to this student (or students). This commitment will entail building a positive relationship, teaching appropriate behavior, and offering continuous behavioral guidance as the weeks and months ahead proceed.

3 After you have identified your difficult student(s) begin with Part 1 and proceed sequentially through the book. For each student you identify you will be building an individualized plan—and it is important that all elements of that plan are addressed as presented.

Build a Student Profile

As you proceed through this workbook you will notice that various pages in each section have been marked "Student File Copy."

These are the pages you will remove, reproduce, add information to, and place in a permanent individual Student File. This file will be your ongoing guide to working more effectively with your student. The file will provide both a roadmap for your future efforts and documentation of what you have accomplished.

At the end of each section of the workbook you will find a review that will help you organize and keep track of the most vital contents of your Student File. You will also find behavior management reminders and information about your next step in working with your difficult student.

You are taking an important step on behalf of a student who needs the help and guidance of an adult who is willing to care. The path won't always be smooth, but you can be assured that by consistently demonstrating your commitment, both you and your student will benefit.

Before you begin:

It is not uncommon to find that excessive disruptive behavior within one class is caused not by a large number of difficult students, but rather by problems in the overall behavior management of the class.

Before you begin using this program with a difficult student, ask yourself these questions:

☐ Do I have clearly defined classroom rules? Have I taught these rules to my students? Do all students know exactly what is expected of them throughout the day?

☐ Do I provide consistent positive reinforcement to students who follow the rules?

☐ Do my students know what positive reinforcement they can expect?

☐ Do I consistently provide consequences when students do not follow the rules? Do they know what will happen the first time they break a rule? The second time? The third time?

☐ Do students know ahead of time the consequences they will receive if they choose to misbehave?

☐ Do I have a clear plan of how I will respond to inappropriate behavior?

☐ Has my behavior management plan been communicated to parents?

☐ Have I taught specific behavior expectations for all the activities students engage in within my classroom?

☐ Do I re-teach behavior expectations as necessary throughout the year?

If you cannot confidently answer yes to all of these questions, you may want to take a closer look at your overall classroom behavior management.

The following resources from Lee Canter will help you create a well-managed, positive classroom environment in which you can teach and students can learn.

Assertive Discipline®—Positive Behavior Management for Today's Classroom

Assertive Discipline® Elementary Workbook

Assertive Discipline® Middle-School Workbook

Assertive Discipline® Secondary Workbook

Part 1

Establish a Positive Relationship with Your Difficult Student

Teachers who are successful with difficult students know that a trusting, positive relationship between student and teacher is the foundation upon which positive behavioral change is built. They understand that difficult students do not view school in the same way that other students do. For these students, school has not been a positive experience. For these students, relationships with teachers have most likely been negative.

Difficult students, therefore, do not intrinsically trust that what teachers ask of them is in their best interest.

If a teacher is to have any impact on a difficult student, he or she must first build trust and a positive relationship with that student. Day in and day out, through words and actions, the teacher must send this message:

> "I'm your teacher. I care about you and I'm going to do everything in my power to help you succeed. I'm here for you.

> "No matter what has happened in the past, this year I want you to succeed."

The ideas presented on the following pages will help you develop positive relationships with difficult students before school begins, at the beginning of the year and throughout the year.

The importance of developing a positive relationship with a difficult student cannot be overemphasized. This relationship is the key to everything you want to accomplish. It is an ongoing goal that will be an integral part of everything you do with the student.

Before School Begins. . .

Make sure that your very first contact with a difficult student is a positive one.

Call the student before school begins.

Most difficult students are accustomed to hearing from school only when problems arise—when a call or note goes home to parents. Calling a student before school begins just to say a welcoming, sincere hello is one of the most powerful steps you can take in letting the student know that you will be on his or her side this year—and that you are committed to doing all you can to ensure success.

Here's what to say:

1 **Introduce yourself.** Tell the student that you are looking forward to having him or her in your class this year—and through the enthusiasm and sincerity in your voice let the student know you mean it.

2 **Ask the student for ideas** about how this school year could be more successful. You may hear something that will help you shape your efforts with this student.

3 **Listen to what the student has to say.** Difficult students are not accustomed to being heard. Demonstrate to your student right from the start that you *will* listen.

4 **Communicate your confidence** that you and the student will work together to have a good year.

Above all, leave the student with positive and confident feelings about the year ahead. Don't be surprised, however, if the student does not respond positively or is uncommunicative. A phone call like this is something the student is not accustomed to. You won't allay all of the student's suspicions and negative feelings with just this one call, but you'll have taken an important first step in building trust.

Sample Phone Call:

"Jason, my name is Mr. Cooper. I'm going to be your English teacher this year. I just wanted to give you a call before school begins to say hi and let you know that I'm looking forward to having you in my class.

"I can see from your file that you've done some interesting writing projects in the past. I think you'll find that our class this year will give you lots of opportunity to flex some creative muscle. One thing you might be interested in is that we're going to write a screenplay for a television show—and that should be lots of fun.

"Jason, as long as I have you on the phone, I'd sure like to hear any ideas you have about what could make this a good year for you. Any suggestions? I'm here to listen if there's anything you'd like to say.

If the student responds, listen. If he or she has nothing to say, or puts you off, don't take it personally. You asked, and that point won't be forgotten.

"Well, I'm really looking forward to the year ahead, Jason, and I want you to feel good about it, too. Enjoy the rest of your vacation and I'll see you on the 8th."

How will this student feel on the way to school the first day? Because his teacher has been positive and encouraging, chances are this student will feel better than he is accustomed to feeling at the start of a new year.

Call the parent before school begins.

Parents of difficult students, like the students themselves, are used to negative interactions with school, not positive ones. A beginning-of-the- year phone call to a parent will communicate that whatever went on in the past, you are committed to doing everything you can to ensure a more successful year for the student.

Follow these guidelines:

1 **Begin with a statement of caring.** Let the parent know that you really are committed to the success of his or her child this year.

2 **Get parental input about the student's experiences the previous year.** Listen to what the parent says, even if he or she is angry and negative. If you are going to help this student, you need to know where his or her parents are coming from, too.

3 **Get parental input on what the child needs from you this year.** The parent may have valuable information that could help you.

4 **Emphasize that the student will be most successful if teacher and parent work together.** Promote the home-school partnership. Let the parent know that he or she is the most important person in the child's life, and that the parent's support, confidence and enthusiasm are the key ingredients in the student's eventual success.

5 **Communicate your confidence** that by working together the child will have a more successful experience at school.

These two phone calls can set the stage for the positive relationship you will be building all year long. When first contact is positive, you will be in a much better position to deal with problems that inevitably will arise.

Use the Phone Call Record Sheet on page 16 to plan and document your calls. Keep the Record Sheet in your Student File.

Phone Call
Record Sheet
Page 16

Build positive relationships at the beginning of the year...

Here's a selection of activities that will help you become better acquainted with your students—and put you in a better position to build positive relationships.

Take Student Interest Inventories.

A Student Interest Inventory, taken at the beginning of the year, is a great way to learn more about all of your students. It's an especially valuable tool for gaining insight into the interests of your difficult student(s). This information will be helpful as you build a positive relationship with the student throughout the year.

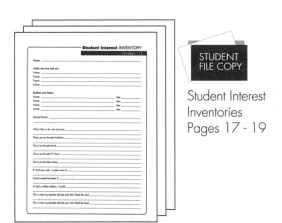

STUDENT FILE COPY

Student Interest Inventories Pages 17 - 19

On pages 17-19 you will find reproducible Student Interest Inventories for grades 1-3, 4-6 and 7-12. Have students fill these out during the first week of school. And remember, a positive relationship is a two-way street. Prepare a "bio" of yourself to pass out to students at the same time. Teachers who let students know that they are "people" too develop much stronger relationships than teachers who remain simply "teachers."

How to Use the Student Interest Inventory to Build Positive Relationships

A Student Interest Inventory will tell you about a student's hobbies, favorite movies, books, TV shows and other likes and dislikes. The more you know about a student, the more effectively you can reach out to him or her.

For example:

- If a student lists drawing or painting as an interest, ask him or her to make some artistic contributions to the decor of the classroom.

- If a student lets you know that he or she has a special interest in a subject, make sure this student becomes the class "expert." Increase the student's self-esteem by asking him or her to contribute information to a class discussion or project.

- If a student lets you know that he or she plays a sport, show up for a game or match.

- If a student is a dancer or actor, make a point of attending a performance.

- If a student lets you know that he or she is employed someplace, stop by to say hello.

Send first-day letters.

Here's an idea for elementary and middle-school classrooms. Write an introductory letter to your students telling about yourself—your hobbies and interests, why you are a teacher, and anything else you'd like to share that will help your students become better acquainted with you.

Leave a copy of the letter on each student's desk. When students arrive at school the first day, ask them to read your letter and then write a letter back to you telling about themselves. Use the reproducible letter form on page 20.

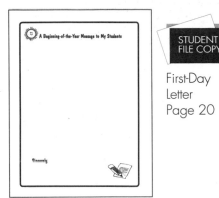

First-Day
Letter
Page 20

Fill out "Someone Special" sheets.

Most students have people in their lives who are special—people they can talk to, vent their anger to, rely on. These special people might include a parent, a friend, a relative or a neighbor. This sheet will let you know who the influential people in a child's life are.

Someone
Special Sheet
Page 21

Create personal posters.

The value of this activity is two-fold: You will learn more about each of your students, and they are given an esteem-building opportunity to share their interests with you and their peers.

Here's what to do:

- Give each student a sheet of poster board.
- Tell students that they are to gather a collection of items that will tell others about themselves, somewhat like an "advertisement about me." Students can collect items such as:

- photographs or illustrations from magazines that signify something important to them
- personal photographs of self, family, pet or friends
- awards or recognitions they have received
- items that represent personal interests, such as a program from a play, concert or sports event
- three-dimensional items that can be affixed to the board, such as collectables (a shell, a coin, a baseball card) or art projects

- Have students create a collage of these items on the poster board. Each Personal Poster should be titled with the student's name and then displayed in the classroom.

Remember to pay special attention to the poster(s) of your difficult student(s). You can learn a lot about the student from what he or she is saying through this project.

Organize a Teacher's Lunch Bunch.

Here's an idea that will help you get better acquainted with all of your students, and will also give you an opportunity to integrate your difficult student(s) into a positive, relaxed group interaction of students and teacher.

At the beginning of the year invite small groups of students to join you on specific days for lunch. Have students bring sack lunches (or trays from the cafeteria) and you can provide dessert. The plan should be for casual conversation and getting acquainted.

Build positive relationships throughout the year...

Building a positive relationship with a difficult student begins before school starts and continues throughout the year. These ideas will help you keep the positive momentum going.

Greet students at the door.

Every day you have a built-in opportunity to say a few personal words of encouragement and recognition to each and every one of your students. How? Simply stand by your door as students enter the classroom. A nod, some special words, a pat on the back or a handshake are often enough to let a student know that you're thinking of him or her. And it's a great way to set a positive tone for the day or period ahead, particularly with difficult students.

Call student after a bad day.

A bad day doesn't feel good to you or to a student. And, unfortunately, it often carries over to the next day and the next. A phone call to the student will help both you and the student put the past in its place and move forward.

Here's how this phone call might sound:

Teacher: Leslie, this is Mr. Foster. I want to talk to you because I feel bad about the difficult day you and I had. It wasn't easy for me to see you so upset, and I know that it wasn't easy for you, either.

Can you give me some idea of what was going on today? Why did you keep getting so upset with Jonathan?

Leslie: I don't know. He's always saying stuff about me and it makes me mad.

Teacher: Then you lose your temper?

Leslie: Yeah. And then I get in trouble. And then I get mad at you.

Teacher: I understand why you'd be angry when Jonathan gets after you, Leslie. And I understand that you'd be mad at me when you get in trouble. So let's do something to solve this. I think maybe a first step would be to move your seat. Would that help if you weren't near Jonathan?

Leslie: I guess. It'd help during class anyway.

Teacher: Good. It would be a start. I want you to be successful in my class, Leslie. And I want to do whatever I can to make that happen. Tomorrow I'll move you and we'll see how the day goes, okay?

Leslie: Sure, I guess.

Teacher: Good. Tomorrow we can start off fresh, and I'm sure you'll have a better day. Get a good rest tonight and I'll see you in the morning.

Make home visits.

A difficult student often has difficult issues in his or her home life to deal with. A home visit can offer an unparalleled opportunity to take a closer look at the student's reality.

Plan how you will build a positive relationship with your student.

15+ Terrific Ways to Build A Positive Relationship

The "15+ Terrific Ways to Build A Positive Relationship" sheet on page 22 contains a list of ideas you can use to build a relationship with a difficult student. It also contains space to add ideas of your own that are particularly applicable to a specific student. Keep this sheet in your Student File as a handy resource.

Use the Relationship-Building Plan on page 23 to plan and document the specific techniques you use with your student throughout the semester or year. Keep this form in your Student File and update it frequently.

15+ Terrific Ways to Build A Positive Relationship
Page 22

Relationship-Building Plan
Page 23

PHONE CALL RECORD SHEET

DATE:

STUDENT NAME:

CLASS/PERIOD:

Phone Call
Record Sheet

Student's name _____

Home phone _____

Parents' names _____

Date of call _____

To whom was the call made? _____

Reason for call: _____

_____

_____

Notes/Comments

_____

_____

_____

_____

Date of call _____

To whom was the call made? _____

Reason for call: _____

_____

_____

Notes/Comments

_____

_____

_____

_____

Date of call _____

To whom was the call made? _____

Reason for call: _____

_____

_____

Notes/Comments

_____

_____

_____

_____

Name _____

Adults who live with me:

Name _____

Name _____

Name _____

Name _____

Brothers and Sisters

Name _____ Age _____

Name _____ Age _____

Name _____ Age _____

Name _____ Age _____

Special friends: _____

_____

What I like to do most at home: _____

_____

These are my favorite hobbies: _____

_____

This is my favorite book: _____

_____

This is my favorite TV show: _____

_____

This is my favorite movie: _____

_____

If I had one wish, I would want to: _____

_____

School would be better if: _____

_____

If I had a million dollars, I would: _____

_____

This is what my teacher did last year that I liked the most: _____

_____

This is what my teacher did last year that I liked the least: _____

_____

Student Interest INVENTORY

Grades 4-6

Name _____

Adults who live with me:

Name _____

Name _____

Name _____

Name _____

Brothers and Sisters

Name _____ Age _____

Name _____ Age _____

Name _____ Age _____

Name _____ Age _____

Special friends: _____

_____

What I like to do most at home: _____

_____

These are my favorite hobbies: _____

_____

This is my favorite book: _____

_____

This is my favorite TV show: _____

_____

This is my favorite movie: _____

_____

If I had one wish, I would want to: _____

_____

School would be better if: _____

_____

If I had a million dollars, I would: _____

_____

This is what my teacher did last year that I liked the most: _____

_____

This is what my teacher did last year that I liked the least: _____

_____

Student Interest INVENTORY

Grades 7-12

Name _____

Brothers and Sisters

Name _____ Age _____
Name _____ Age _____
Name _____ Age _____
Name _____ Age _____

Special friends _____   _____

_____   _____

What I like to do most at home: _____

_____

These are my favorite hobbies: _____

_____

These are my favorites:

book: _____ TV show: _____

movie: _____ food: _____

singer: _____ song: _____

If I had one wish, I would want to: _____

School would be better if: _____

If I had a million dollars, I would _____

This is what one of my teachers did last year that I liked the most: _____

_____

_____

_____

This is what one of my teachers did last year that I liked the least: _____

_____

_____

_____

_____

A Beginning-of-the-Year Message to My Students

Sincerely,

Someone Special

My name is _____

One person who is special in my life is _____
This person is special to me because _____
_____
_____

Another person who is special to me is _____
This person is special because _____
_____
_____

Another person who is special to me is _____
This person is special because _____
_____
_____

Someone Special

My name is _____

One person who is special in my life is _____
This person is special to me because _____
_____
_____

Another person who is special to me is _____
This person is special because _____
_____
_____

Another person who is special to me is _____
This person is special because _____
_____
_____

15+ Terrific Ways to Build

a Positive Relationship with a Student

1 Call the student before school begins.

2 Send a birthday greeting.

3 Make a positive phone call.

4 Visit the student at his or her place of employment (if permitted).

5 Attend a sports event in which the student is participating.

6 Attend a concert or theatrical event in which the student is participating.

7 Share books about a subject in which the student is interested.

8 Make a friendly home visit.

9 Invite the student to lunch.

10 Greet students at the door.

11 Send a positive note home to the student.

12 Display the student's artwork or creative writing in the classroom.

13 Phone home when the student is ill.

14 Listen to the student.

15 Call student after a bad day.

Ideas of your own:

16 _____

17 _____

18 _____

19 _____

20 _____

STUDENT FILE COPY

DATE:

STUDENT NAME:
CLASS/PERIOD:

Relationship-Building Plan

Relationship-Building Plan for _____
STUDENT'S NAME

Throughout the year you will utilize many different techniques as you continue to build a positive relationship with a difficult student. Keep a record of techniques you have used, or plan to use, and document the ongoing results. Use this record to evaluate past efforts and plan future ones.

STRATEGY	RESULTS

DATE:

STUDENT FILE COPY

RELATIONSHIP-BUILDING PLAN

STUDENT FILE COPY Student File Update

At this point your Student File should contain the following:

- ✔ Phone Call Record Sheet
- ✔ Relationship-Building Plan
- ✔ Student Interest Inventory
- ✔ 15+ Ways to Develop Positive Relationships with Students
- ☐ Primary Need Worksheet
- ☐ Goals Sheet
- ☐ Behavior Profile
- ☐ Lesson Plan(s) for Teaching Appropriate Behavior
- ☐ Providing Positive Support Cue Card
- ☐ Positive Phone Call Planner
- ☐ Redirecting Technique Cue Card

- ☐ Cue Card for Providing Consequences
- ☐ Cue Card for Defusing Covert Confrontations
- ☐ Cue Card for Defusing Overt Confrontations
- ☐ Cue Card for Conducting a Problem-Solving Conference
- ☐ Problem-Solving Conference Worksheet
- ☐ Any documentation pertaining to an Individualized Behavior Plan you are using with the student.
- ☐ Substitute's Plan

Reminders

- Continue to document all phone calls to student and parents. These records will be important to have as you work with the student throughout the year.

- Refer to the Student Interest Inventory as you plan relationship-building activities and strategies.

- Did you ever think you could easily give positive support to each and every student each and every day? Get into

the habit of greeting all of your students at the door each day and that's exactly what will happen.

- Don't forget to call a student after a bad day. You'll both feel better and the relationship you are building will be improved.

- Whenever you think of or hear about a great relationship-building idea add it to your "15+" sheet.

Your Next Step

In the next section of this workbook you will identify the specific unmet need that is prompting your difficult student to choose to behave inappropriately. This will be your first step toward individualizing your behavior management efforts with this student.

Part 2

Identify Your Difficult Student's Primary Need

Research has shown that difficult students act out and misbehave because of strong needs that are not adequately being met in their lives.

- **Some students are difficult because they need attention.**

- **Some students are difficult because they need firmer limits.**

- **Some students are difficult because they need more motivation.**

As a result, difficult students need something from you that your other students don't need. They need a teacher to recognize that real unmet needs are prompting them to choose behaviors that are not in their best interest. They need a teacher who will give them what they need to *appropriately* fulfill these needs.

Until you accurately identify *why* a student misbehaves you cannot accurately identify what the student needs from you and what steps you can take to effectively meet the student's needs so that he or she will be less disruptive and more successful.

To clarify this concept, the profiles on the next pages will illustrate the attributes of the student who needs attention, the student who needs firmer limits and the student who needs motivation.

Shawna:
A Student Who Needs Attention

"Shawna is like a tornado in my classroom. She's up and down, up and down all day long. I never know where she'll touch down next! One minute she's at the water fountain, the next minute she's at another student's desk. Usually, however, she's somewhere near me, trying to get my attention for one thing or another. Even when she's in her seat, though, she's always asking questions, calling out to me, adding silly noises or commentary to my lessons. With Shawna it's not so much that she's defiant, confrontational or disrespectful. It's just that her constant disruptions take up far too much of my time and her continual attention-getting behavior annoys me so much."

Students like Shawna need attention from peers and from their teachers and they will do whatever it takes to get that attention. What usually happens is that they get that attention for disruptive behavior and are thus motivated to continue the inappropriate behavior.

Robert:
A Student Who Needs Firmer Limits

"I can't ask Robert to do a thing without getting a confrontational attitude back. If I tell him to put his books away he glares at me. And does nothing. If I direct him to work on an assignment he argues with me—and makes it very clear that he doesn't care a thing about what I say. Robert always has to be the big shot in the classroom. He has to show the other kids that he's the boss, not me. This goes on all the time—I get angry at him, and I can't seem to help it."

Students like Robert need firm limits, something they probably aren't getting at home or at school. Because of this, these students constantly need to test limits and confront the teacher's authority.

Kerrie:
A Student Who Needs Motivation

"Just getting Kerrie to begin an assignment is a big deal. She'll sharpen her pencil, write and erase her name over and over again—anything to avoid trying to do the work. If I ask her to get to work she'll always answer that she can't do it. I try to be understanding and helpful but if I push her too hard she'll cry and then I have a real problem on my hands. It's as though she's so scared to fail that she won't even take the first step. I'm so frustrated with her because nothing I do seems to have any effect. She just won't do her work—and I know that it's work she's capable of doing."

Students like Kerrie have no self-confidence. Well-meaning teachers often offer sympathetic but ineffective responses to these students, responses that only demonstrate that they really don't have high expectations either. By patronizing and placating the student, the teacher is actually enabling failure. The end result? The student gets out of doing work and the teacher is increasingly frustrated.

The need for more attention.

The need for firmer limits.

The need for more motivation.

When teachers respond ineffectively to these behaviors they are often in fact fulfilling the student's need, but in a way that does not help the student and instead further encourages inappropriate behavior.

> It's important to remember that difficult students continue to engage in inappropriate behaviors *because they get something from it.*

What need is your difficult student attempting to fulfill?

The following activity will guide you in identifying your student's primary need.

Here's what to do:

1 First, complete the "Identifying a Difficult Student's Primary Need" sheet on pages 29 - 30.

Does the student need more attention, firmer limits or more motivation? Before you can work effectively with your difficult student you need to find out what is motivating him or her to choose inappropriate behavior. Completing this worksheet and identifying your student's need is the first step in individualizing a plan you will use to help the student be more successful.

2 Then complete the appropriate "Goals" sheet (pages 31, 32 or 33) for the student.

Once you've identified a student's primary need, you can begin to focus on the general goals you will have for working with this particular student. The goals contained on this sheet will serve as a roadmap to guide you as you plan strategies for helping him or her choose more appropriate behavior.

As you continue to work with this student you may wish to add more individualized goals in the space provided.

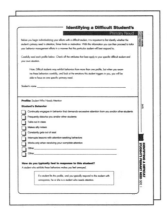

Identifying
a Difficult
Student's
Need
Pages 29 - 30

Goals Sheet
Pages 31 - 33

Identifying a Difficult Student's
Primary Need

Before you begin individualizing your efforts with a difficult student, it is important to first identify whether the student's primary need is attention, firmer limits or motivation. With this information you can then proceed to tailor your behavior management efforts in a manner that this particular student will best respond to.

Carefully read each profile below. Check off the attributes that best apply to your specific difficult student and your own situation.

> Note: Difficult students may exhibit behaviors from more than one profile, but when you examine these behaviors carefully, and look at the emotions this student triggers in you, you will be able to focus on one specific primary need.

Student's name _____

Profile: Student Who Needs Attention

Student's Behavior

- ☐ Continually engages in behavior that demands excessive attention from you and/or other students
- ☐ Frequently disturbs you and/or other students
- ☐ Talks out in class
- ☐ Makes silly noises
- ☐ Constantly gets out of seat
- ☐ Interrupts lessons with attention-seeking behaviors
- ☐ Works only when receiving your complete attention
- ☐ Other_____
- ☐ Other_____

How do you typically feel in response to this student?

A student who exhibits these behaviors makes you feel *annoyed*.

> If a student fits this profile, and you typically respond to this student with annoyance, he or she is a student who needs attention.

STUDENT FILE COPY

DATE:

Profile: Student Who Needs Firmer Limits

Student's Behavior

☐ Constantly challenges you or other students

☐ Talks back to you in front of other students

☐ Argues

☐ Lies

☐ Verbally or physically fights with other students

☐ Refuses to do what is asked

☐ Is in a power struggle with you

☐ Other _____

☐ Other _____

How do you typically feel in response to this student?

A student who exhibits these behaviors makes you feel *angry*.

> If a student fits this profile, and you typically respond to this student with anger, he or she is a student who needs firmer limits.

Profile: Student Who Needs Motivation

Student's Behavior

☐ Makes excuses for why work cannot be done

☐ Will not attempt to do academic work

☐ If an attempt is made, the student will give up very easily

☐ Other _____

☐ Other _____

How do you typically feel in response to this student?

A student who exhibits these behaviors makes you feel *frustrated*.

> If a student fits this profile, and you typically respond to this student with frustration, he or she is a student who needs motivation.

STUDENT NAME:

CLASS/PERIOD:

Now that you've identified the primary need of your student, here is the overall goal that you will keep in mind as you begin to implement more individualized, specialized techniques.

GOAL for _____:

STUDENT'S NAME

Give massive amounts of positive attention for appropriate behavior.

The student who needs attention will take whatever kind of attention he or she can get from you—good or bad. In order to help this student succeed, you need to plan to give him or her the maximum amount of positive attention in the shortest amount of time, so the need for negative consequences comes only as a last resort.

When you give lots of attention for appropriate behavior, and minimal attention for negative behavior, your attention-seeking student will soon learn how best to get what he or she wants.

NOTES: _____
_____
_____
_____
_____
_____
_____
_____
_____
_____
_____

Now that you've identified the primary need of your student, here is the overall goal that you will keep in mind as you begin to implement more individualized, specialized techniques.

GOAL for _____ :

STUDENT'S NAME

Provide very firm and consistent limits.

This student wants power and control. Therefore, he or she needs to be provided very, very firm and very consistent limits in a non-confrontational way. You must always work with this student in a way that allows him or her to save face in the classroom—even when you're setting limits.

NOTES: _____

_____

_____

_____

_____

_____

_____

_____

_____

_____

_____

_____

_____

_____

GOAL FOR THE STUDENT
Who Needs Firmer Limits

STUDENT FILE COPY

DATE:

STUDENT NAME:

CLASS/PERIOD:

STUDENT NAME:

CLASS/PERIOD:

DATE:

STUDENT FILE COPY

GOAL FOR THE STUDENT
Who Needs Motivation

Now that you've identified the primary need of your student, here is the overall goal that you will keep in mind as you begin to implement more individualized, specialized techniques.

GOAL for _____ :
                                    STUDENT'S NAME

Focus all behavioral efforts toward getting the student to do work.

Above all, let this student know that you have confidence in his or her ability to do the work. Always maintain high expectations—and let the student *know* you have high expectations. If need be, break assignments down to manageable parts and strive to get the student starting and completing assignments with the rest of the class. Offer this student the maximum amount of motivation you possibly can to encourage him or her to do any kind of work possible. All corrective actions taken with this student must be focused toward getting him or her to do the work.

If the work isn't done in class, it *must* be completed at another time.

NOTES: _____

_____

_____

_____

_____

_____

_____

_____

_____

_____

STUDENT FILE COPY

Student File Update

At this point your Student File should contain the following:

☑ Phone Call Record Sheet

☑ Relationship-Building Plan

☑ Student Interest Inventory

☑ 15+ Ways to Develop Positive Relationships with Students

☑ Primary Need Worksheet

☑ Goals Sheet

☐ Behavior Profile

☐ Lesson Plan(s) for Teaching Appropriate Behavior

☐ Providing Positive Support Cue Card

☐ Positive Phone Call Planner

☐ Redirecting Technique Cue Card

☐ Cue Card for Providing Consequences

☐ Cue Card for Defusing Covert Confrontations

☐ Cue Card for Defusing Overt Confrontations

☐ Cue Card for Conducting a Problem-Solving Conference

☐ Problem-Solving Conference Worksheet

☐ Any documentation pertaining to an Individualized Behavior Plan you are using with the student.

☐ Substitute's Plan

Reminders

- The Student File is an active part of your daily efforts with a difficult student. Keep it close by to remind yourself of your relationship-building plans with this student.

  Ask yourself at the end of each week, "What did I do this week to further build a positive relationship with this student? What will I do next week?"

- Once you have identified your student's primary need, stay focused on that need throughout all classroom interactions. Keep in mind your general goal with this student and let that goal guide your responses to the student's behavior. As you proceed through this workbook you will be introduced to specific techniques that you can use to more effectively meet the student's primary need.

Your Next Step ▶ ▶ ▶

The next step you will take with your difficult student will be to teach appropriate behavior.

Part 3

Teach Appropriate Behavior

You're taking steps to build a positive relationship with your difficult student.

You've identified his or her primary need and focused on your overall goal for the student.

Now, what specifically can you do right away to help your student improve his or her behavior in your classroom?

First, you will *teach* your student the behavior you expect.

Why teach behavior? The truth is that many difficult students simply do not know how to behave or they may not understand your expectations for different activities. If they are ever going to be successful in your class, they need to be taught, or retaught, appropriate behavior for the specific activities in which they behave inappropriately.

To help your student be more successful, you need to identify the exact circumstances in which he or she behaves inappropriately.

The best way to define which behaviors to focus on is to develop a Behavior Profile on your student. This profile includes the following information:

1 **The activities during which the student is noncompliant.**

2 **The specific problem behaviors that occur during those activities.**

3 **The appropriate behaviors you want the student to engage in.**

Follow these steps when developing a Behavior Profile on your student:

STEP ONE: Determine when problems occur.

To teach a student appropriate behavior, you first need to find out during which activities the student is actually behaving inappropriately. (Most difficult students really don't misbehave all the time, even though it may seem that way to you.) Based on the student's primary need, you will find that certain classroom activities throughout the day lend themselves to inappropriate, noncompliant behavior.

Think about your own difficult student, and his or her need, and see if the following examples are accurate.

A student who needs attention is likely to be noncompliant when he or she can't get your attention. For example:

- when you're with a group and the student is supposed to be working independently

- when you are working one-on-one with another student

A student who needs firm limits is likely to be noncompliant when you ask him or her to do something or function in an unstructured situation. For example:

- during transitions

- when working in cooperative learning groups

- when asked to follow any direction

A student who needs motivation is likely to be noncompliant when asked to do academic work.

Observe your student for a day or two. On the Behavior Profile (page 40) write down the activities during which noncompliant behaviors occurred.

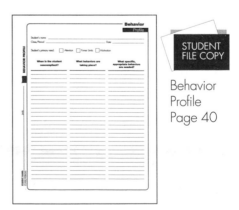

Behavior
Profile
Page 40

For example:

Behavior Profile: David

When is the student noncompliant?	What behaviors are taking place?	What specific, appropriate behaviors are needed?
Independent seatwork

Class discussion

Groups | | |

STEP TWO: Define the problem behavior.

Fill out the second column of the Behavior Profile. What noncompliant behaviors are taking place? Be specific. List only specific, observable behaviors (such as out of seat, shouts out, hits classmates). Vague observations such as "doesn't act nice" or "has a bad attitude" give you no real information.

For example:

Behavior Profile: David

When is the student noncompliant?	What behaviors are taking place?	What specific, appropriate behaviors are needed?
Independent seatwork	Argues when asked to work, talks, gets out of seat	
Class discussion	Speaks without raising hand, disruptive remarks, out of seat	
Groups	Out of seat, does not work with group, distracts others, disruptive conversation	

STEP THREE: Plan what you want the student to do.

What specific appropriate behaviors are needed for the student to be successful? Plan exactly how you expect the student to behave during the activities you listed. Write your expectations in the third column on the Behavior Profile. You will use this information to teach appropriate behavior to your student.

For example:

Behavior Profile: David

When is the student noncompliant?	What behaviors are taking place?	What specific, appropriate behaviors are needed?
Independent seatwork	Argues when asked to work, talks, gets out of seat	Begin assignment when given direction, eyes on work, no talking, raise hand if help is needed
Class discussion	Speaks without raising hand, disruptive remarks, out of seat	Raise hand to speak or ask a question, stay in seat, speak only when called upon
Groups	Out of seat, does not work with group, distracts others, disruptive conversation	Stay in seat, keep hands to self, work only on assignment, talk only about the assignment

By reviewing your student's Behavior Profile, you can see at a glance those activities during which he or she is noncompliant. You can also see the specific behaviors he or she needs to be taught.

Teach the Appropriate Behavior

When you take the time to teach a difficult student appropriate behavior you are not only proactively preventing problems from continuing, but you are also showing the student that you care enough to do what needs to be done to help him or her succeed.

On pages 41, 42, and 43 you will find lesson plans and guidelines for teaching appropriate behavior to students in grades K-3, 4-6 and 7-12. Fill out a lesson plan for the behavior you are going to teach. Use this as a guide when teaching your student and as documentation of what you have done.

Note: Do not attempt to teach behavior for all activities at one time. Start with the one that is most disruptive to you and focus on it first. Later, as the student's behavior improves in one area, you can teach appropriate behavior for another.

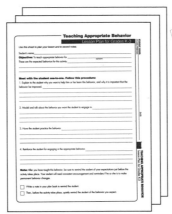

Lesson Plans for
Teaching
Appropriate Behavior
Grades K-3, Page 41
Grades 4-6, Page 42
Grades 7-12, Page 43

Refer to pages 87-89 of the Succeeding With Difficult Students *text for scenarios that demonstrate how to teach appropriate behavior to students grades K-3, grades 4-6 and grades 7-12.*

Behavior
Profile

STUDENT FILE COPY

Student's name _____

Class/Period _____ Date _____

Student's primary need: ☐ Attention   ☐ Firmer Limits   ☐ Motivation

When is the student noncompliant?	What behaviors are taking place?	What specific, appropriate behaviors are needed?

Teaching Appropriate Behavior
Lesson Plan for Grades K-3

Use this sheet to plan your lesson and to record notes.

Student's name_____

Objective: To teach appropriate behavior for _____
                                                                                            ACTIVITY

These are the expected behaviors for this activity: _____

_____

_____

Meet with the student one-to-one. Follow this procedure:

1. Explain to the student why you want to help him or her learn this behavior, and why it is important that the behavior be improved. _____

_____

_____

_____

2. Model and talk about the behavior you want the student to engage in. _____

_____

_____

_____

3. Have the student practice the behavior. _____

_____

_____

_____

4. Reinforce the student for engaging in the appropriate behavior. _____

_____

_____

_____

Note: After you have taught this behavior, be sure to remind the student of your expectations just before the activity takes place. Your student will need consistent encouragement and reminders if he or she is to make permanent behavior changes.

☐ Write a note in your plan book to remind the student.

☐ Then, before the activity takes place, quietly remind the student of the behavior you expect.

STUDENT
FILE COPY

DATE:

Teaching Appropriate Behavior

Lesson Plan for Grades 4-6

Use this sheet to plan your lesson and to record notes.

Student's name_____

Objective: To teach appropriate behavior for_____
                                                                            ACTIVITY
These are the expected behaviors for this activity: _____
_____

Meet with the student one-to-one. Follow this procedure:

1. Explain to the student why you are meeting with him/her. _____
_____
_____
_____

2. Explain the rationale for why the student should engage in the appropriate behavior. _____
_____
_____
_____

3. Tell the student the exact behavior you want him or her to engage in._____
_____
_____
_____

4. Before ending the meeting, have the student repeat or write down the behaviors you expect.
_____
_____
_____

Note: After you have taught this behavior, be sure to remind the student of your expectations just before the activity takes place. Your student will need consistent encouragement and reminders if he or she is to make permanent behavior changes.

☐ Write a note in your plan book to remind the student.

☐ Then, before the activity takes place, quietly remind the student of the behavior you expect.

Teaching Appropriate Behavior

Lesson Plan for Grades 7-12

Use this sheet to plan your lesson and to record notes.

Student's name _____

Objective: To teach appropriate behavior for _____
                                                  ACTIVITY

These are the expected behaviors for this activity:_____

_____

_____

Meet one-to-one with the student. Follow this procedure:

In a very matter-of-fact manner specify the exact behaviors you expect. _____

_____

_____

_____

_____

_____

_____

_____

_____

_____

_____

_____

_____

_____

_____

_____

_____

_____

Note: After you have taught this behavior, be sure to remind the student of your expectations just before the activity takes place. Your student will need consistent encouragement and reminders if he or she is to make permanent behavior changes.

☐   Write a note in your plan book to remind the student.

☐   Then, before the activity takes place, quietly remind the student of the behavior you expect.

Student File Update

STUDENT FILE COPY

At this point your Student File should contain the following:

- ✓ Phone Call Record Sheet
- ✓ Relationship-Building Plan
- ✓ Student Interest Inventory
- ✓ 15+ Ways to Develop Positive Relationships with Students
- ✓ Primary Need Worksheet
- ✓ Goals Sheet
- ✓ Behavior Profile
- ✓ Lesson Plan(s) for Teaching Appropriate Behavior
- ☐ Providing Positive Support Cue Card
- ☐ Positive Phone Call Planner
- ☐ Redirecting Technique Cue Card

- ☐ Cue Card for Providing Consequences
- ☐ Cue Card for Defusing Covert Confrontations
- ☐ Cue Card for Defusing Overt Confrontations
- ☐ Cue Card for Conducting a Problem-Solving Conference
- ☐ Problem-Solving Conference Worksheet
- ☐ Any documentation pertaining to an Individualized Behavior Plan you are using with the student.
- ☐ Substitute's Plan

Reminders

- The younger the student, the more crucial it is to actually teach and reteach him or her the appropriate behaviors you expect.

  Reinforce and remind often. Building new behavior habits takes repetition!

- Your goal is to stop problems before they begin. Be proactive. Remind students of the behavior you expect before they have an opportunity to choose inappropriate behavior. It's not cheating—it's giving them an opportunity to succeed.

- Succeeding with a difficult student is an ongoing process, not an endeavor that has a clear end in sight. When your student's behavior in one activity has improved, go back and teach behavior for another.

Your Next Step

Once you have taught your student the specific behaviors you expect for an activity, you must focus your efforts on giving positive support when he or she chooses to behave appropriately. The reinforcement you give for appropriate behavior, and the manner in which you give it, will have a tremendous impact on the student's eventual success.

Part 4

Providing Positive Support

If you are ever going to change a difficult student's behavior, it is your positive interactions that will have the most powerful and lasting effect. Every day that you take the time to warmly greet a student, inquire about something that interests him or her, or make that special effort to show the student that your interest is more than superficial, you are building that all-important bond between teacher and difficult student called **trust**.

Because so many difficult students have home and school backgrounds filled with negativity, they often have very low self-esteem. It is critical that you change this negative spiral by providing these students with daily doses of positive support and encouragement. When you demonstrate your confidence in and high expectations for these students, they have a new incentive to succeed.

How Positive Are You?

Self-evaluation Activity

Building relationships and providing positive support are the keys to succeeding with difficult

P.S.Q.
Test
Page 59

students. If you are interested in discovering how well you positively reinforce your students, take the "P.S.Q." test on page 59. Throughout one time period (math lesson, class period, time from recess to lunch), use the chart to keep track of the times a difficult student misbehaves and the times that you positively reinforce the student for choosing appropriate behavior. After the period, tally the numbers. Your positives should equal or surpass the number of disruptions. Read on to find out why.

The Power of Praise

The most effective positive reinforcer you can use is verbal praise. Focusing on what a difficult student has done right (instead of what he or she has done wrong) will help motivate the student to behave appropriately.

Praise must be sincere and geared toward the need of the individual student. Younger students, especially attention-seekers, enjoy receiving praise given in front of the entire class. Many older students, however, would be embarrassed by this type of praise. A quiet remark, a subtle nod or smile, or a positive comment discreetly written on a note will get your positive message across without embarrassing the student.

The Power of Positive Recognition

Besides praise, most students respond positively to awards, rewards and special privileges. The beauty of this kind of reinforcement is the variety of ways this recognition can be given to students. Throughout this chapter, you will be introduced to many ways of recognizing a difficult student for making good behavior choices.

Why is positive recognition so important with the difficult student? Studies have found that positive support is the only way to effectively change behavior. As you consider positives for your own student, keep this in mind: The more serious a student's problems have been, the more that student needs to receive increased praise and positive recognition from you. A rule of thumb with these students is the more constant the disruptions and the more severe the emotional or organic problem, the more frequent the need is for praise and positive support.

Planning Is the Key

Teachers who provide massive and consistent positive attention to difficult students—at the right times and in a manner that best meets the student's needs—do not do so by chance. They set goals and then plan how to meet these goals.

1   To start the planning process, you must first look at the Behavior Profile of your difficult student.

2   Check the profile to note the activities during which the student misbehaves.

3   Now, check the specific inappropriate behaviors the student engages in.

4.   Finally, review the specific appropriate behaviors the student needs to be taught and given positive recognition for.

By reviewing the Behavior Profile in this manner, you will know at a glance the exact appropriate behavior you need to teach the student and what time during the school day you'll need to increase your use of positives with the student.

Once you know when to target your positive support, you must set goals for yourself to deliver that support.

Go for the Goal

A day in class, or a period, goes by quickly and it's all too easy to intend to give positive support and then not get around to it. Try these simple hints to keep on track.

• Pocket Positives

Once you have determined your goal for positives (for example, 10 times a day), place that number of pennies in your right pocket. Each time you positively recognize the student's appropriate behavior, move one penny from the right pocket to the left. When all the pennies have been moved, you'll know that you have reached your goal.

• Post-It™ Positives

Jot your difficult student's name on a Post-It™ note. Next to the name make an X for each time you plan to positively reinforce the student. Place the Post-It™ in a convenient place—on your desk, on your gradebook or a textbook, on the chalkboard, etc. Each time you positively recognize the student, circle one of the X's. When all are circled, you'll know you've reached your goal.

• Pencil Positives

Determine the number of times you plan to positively reinforce a particular student and place that many pens, pencils or markers in a container on your desk. Whenever you give positive recognition, remove one of them from the container. When they are all gone, congratulate yourself on reaching your goal.

• Plan Book Positives

Reproduce the sheet on page 60 for elementary school or the sheet on page 61 for middle and secondary school. Each sheet should accommodate a week's worth of positives.

Here's how it works:

For each day (or period), write the name of each difficult student and list numerals indicating the number of positives you plan on giving to each student that day. Staple the sheet into your plan book. Throughout the day as you give positive recognition to these students, circle the numbers on the sheet. If you circle all the numbers, you've reached your goal.

Positives
Planner
Pages 60 - 61

Note: When you are planning for your lessons, plan for the positive support you will give your difficult students. In your lesson plan book, write notes that will cue you to meet your goals during specific times of the day or during specific activities.

For example:

Subject:	Social Studies
MONDAY	All groups cooperatively solve problem on pg. 98.
	Homework: Questions 8-16, p. 101
	*Kirk: Praise appropriate behavior during groups
	(10 positives today)

Throughout the day, keep track of meeting your positives goal by putting pen or pencil dots by the student's name.

Praise Prompters

Forget the string around your finger. Try these techniques for reminding yourself to give positive recognition.

- **Clock Cues**
Reproduce one of the "Clock Cue" signs (pages 62 and 63) and place it near the clock in your classroom. Whenever you glance at the clock, it will remind you that the time is always right to look for good behavior.

- **Watch Reminders**
If you wear a wristwatch, simply place a small sticker dot on the watch face. Throughout the day, whenever you look at your watch, you'll be reminded that the time to be positive is "ticking" away.

Clock Cue
Page 62

Clock Cue
Page 63

• Positive Signs

Post these positive signs (pages 64-65) all around your classroom—on the door, the closet, next to the calendar, near the chalkboard. Then start moving. Don't just stay seated at your desk—stay in motion! Move around the classroom looking for good behavior. When you spot good behavior, comment on it.

Look for Positives
POSITIVE, POSITIVE!
PLAN to be
POSITIVE

Positive
Signs
Page 64

One-to-One Praise
THUMBS UP!
Praise phrase begins with
"YOU" instead of "I"

Positive
Signs
Page 65

Praise Pointers

How you praise difficult students is as important as the fact that you do praise them. An attention-seeking student needs to receive praise in a different manner than a student who needs firmer limits.

On pages 66-68 you will find Cue Cards containing guidelines for praising students who need attention, students who need firmer limits, and students who need motivation. Reproduce the appropriate Cue Card for your student and place it in the Student File. Use the "Notes" space to record any information you might want to keep about the effectiveness of these techniques with your student.

CueCard
Providing Positive Support
for the Student Who
Needs Attention, Page 66
Needs Firmer Limits, Page 67
Needs Motivation, Page 68

Positive Notes and Phone Calls

A personal note or phone call from you to a student can have a powerful impact on your relationship-building efforts. Students feel that their behavior efforts are appreciated and are proud to share these accomplishments with their family. Positive notes and phone calls to difficult students should be used consistently throughout the year.

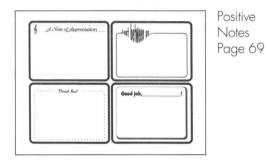

Positive Notes Page 69

Positive Notes Page 70

Use the selection of positive notes on pages 69-70 to deliver your encouraging words. As always, keep the need of the student in mind when choosing your words.

Here's an example of a positive note to a student needing attention:

Dear Emilio:

Just a note to let you know that your input and cooperation during today's science group was appreciated. Your knowledge of machines helped the other members of your group more fully understand the basics of physics. Working together, your group will have an outstanding presentation for the upcoming science fair.

Sincerely,

Mr. Weinberg

The teacher gave this student lots of attention and specifics, even in a note!

Here's an example of a positive note to a student needing firmer limits:

Dear Judy:

You came to class today ready to work and prepared for the test. You're on your way to a great week!

Sincerely,

Mrs. Sanderson

The teacher gave this student praise, but in a brief and matter-of-fact manner. She didn't go overboard, but the student will hear her loud and clear.

Here's an example of a positive note to a student needing motivation:

Dear Linda,

Today you completed the entire project—all by yourself. You should be very proud of this accomplishment. Let's try the "chunking" technique again with tomorrow's math paper.

Great job!

Sincerely,

Mr. Walker

The teacher's praise to this student is tied to her academic achievement of the day. To further encourage the student, he also gives a suggestion for continuing the success the next day.

Fantastic Phone Calls

An unexpected positive phone call to a difficult student can have a very positive effect on your relationship with the student. But be prepared before you dial. Jot down a few specifics you want to compliment the student on. Don't be upset or disheartened if the student doesn't appear to be out-wardly excited or enthusiastic during the call. Your positive message will be heard, and that's your goal in making the call.

Positive Phone Call Planning Sheet Page 71

Use the Positive Phone Call Planning Sheet on page 71 to jot down your notes. Also record any comments the student might make during the conversation.

Here's what a positive phone call to a student who needs attention might sound like:

"Emilio? This is Mr. Weinberg. I wanted to give you a quick call tonight to say how pleased I was with the way you worked in your science group today. Your contributions were extremely helpful to the overall outcome of the project. I appreciated being able to work with the other groups while you and your group members worked cooperatively on your project. Learning how to work within a group will be an important asset after you graduate and get a job."

Here's what a positive phone call to a student who needs firm limits might sound like:

"Judy? This is Mrs. Sanderson. I didn't get a chance to tell you how much you impressed me today. You came to class ready to work. And by the looks of today's quiz results, you put a lot of effort into studying for the test. All I can say is 'Great job.'"

Here's what a positive phone call to a student who needs motivation might sound like:

"Hello, Linda? This is Mr. Walker. I wanted to call you tonight and offer my congratulations on a job well done today. The "chunking" technique that we tried with today's assignment appears to be working wonderfully. You did a great job, so let's try the technique again tomorrow on your math paper. Please tell your parents about this call. I want to share your good news."

Positive Combinations
POSITIVE NOTES & PHONE CALLS

Here's a great way to double the impact of your positive support. Combine tracking charts with positive notes and phone calls!

Great Day Trackers

This reproducible page contains a week's worth of tracking charts and daily positive notes. Reproduce the page and give it to the student. Throughout the day when you see the student behaving appropriately, write your initials in one of the tracking boxes. When the student reaches his or her daily goal (from 5 to 10 positives) write a positive note in the box. Cut off the day's tracking chart and send home to parents.

The charts on page 72 are appropriate for students who need attention and students who need firmer limits. The charts on page 73 have been specially designed for students who need motivation.

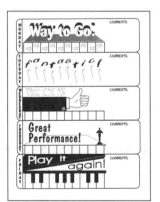

Great Day Tracker Page 72

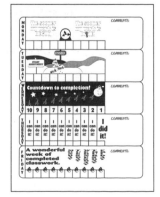

Great Day Tracker Page 73

Terrific Behavior Tear-Offs

These tracking charts hold the promise of a positive note, positive phone call or surprise reward. Reproduce a sheet for your student. Cut off the first strip and tape it to the student's desk, to the inside of the student's notebook, or onto your own desk. When you see the student behaving appropriately, make an X through a letter in the phrase GREAT DAY. When all letters have been marked, provide the positive pictured at the end of the tracking strip. Use the tracking strips in the order seen on the page. In other words, send home positive notes before phoning the parents. And save the surprise tracker to use after a designated period of positive behavior.

Terrific Behavior Tear-Offs Page 74

Special Privileges for Positive Behavior

Special privileges are powerful reinforcers to use with a difficult student because they can be individualized to match a student's interests *and* they are something that only you can give to the student. This is especially important in middle and secondary school when awards may seem too juvenile for some of your students.

The positive relationship you are developing with your student will help you determine the privileges that will be most meaningful to them. The better you know your student, the better able you will be to choose the best privileges for him or her.

Note: It is very important that you give your student privileges that he or she can successfully handle. For example, don't bestow the privilege of running errands to a student who needs constant supervision.

Here are some suggestions for special privileges:

Elementary

- Be a class monitor
- Care for the class pet
- Sit at the teacher's desk
- Choose a game for the class to play
- Get a lunch line "cut coupon"
- Have lunch with the teacher
- Take attendance for the day
- Sit in a different seat for a day

Middle/Secondary

- Sit by a friend for one period
- Take one problem off a test
- Receive extra computer time
- "Homework Postponement" coupon (allows student to postpone turning in a homework assignment one day)
- Create artwork to be displayed in class
- Lunch with teacher

Positive Combinations

SPECIAL PRIVILEGES

Tracking charts that include special privilege coupons are great motivators for younger and older students alike.

Here's how to use them:

To make your positive support as meaningful as possible, allow your student to choose the special-privilege coupon he or she wants to work toward.

On pages 75-79 you will find a collection of reproducible Special Privilege Coupons. Select coupons that are age appropriate for your student, or create your own with the open-ended coupons that are included.

Duplicate the coupon and tape to the student's desk. Initial, mark or stamp the tracking chart when the student displays appropriate behavior. When the chart is filled, the student is awarded the special privilege shown on the coupon.

Note: When a student is first learning appropriate behavior, it is a good idea to positively reinforce good habits more frequently—and enable the student to earn the reward more quickly. Use tracking sheets with five or ten spaces at first. After a few weeks, lengthen the time a student must behave appropriately before receiving a reward.

Special Privilege Coupons Page 75

Special Privilege Coupons Page 77

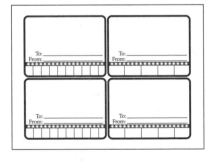

Open-Ended Special Privilege Coupons Page 76

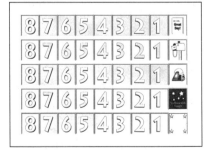

Special Privilege Coupons Page 78

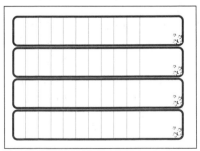

Open-Ended Special Privilege Coupons Page 79

Classwide Positive Recognition

Peer pressure can work very effectively in steering a difficult student toward more appropriate behavior. Some difficult students seem to relish antagonizing and irritating the teacher, but few want to incur the wrath of their fellow classmates. Use this knowledge to help the difficult student behave.

Start a classwide positive reinforcement system.

Here's how such a system works:

1 Offer your students a classwide reward for good behavior, for example, a party at the end of the week, free time on Friday, or a half hour of music. (The reward, of course, should be age appropriate.)

2 Explain to your students that for everyone to receive the reward they will need to earn, as a class, (for example) 50 points.

3 To earn points, tell students that anytime you spot *any one of them* engaging in appropriate behavior, following directions or following the rules of the classroom, you will give the whole class a point. This <u>does not</u> mean the entire class has to be following the rules. It means that you will recognize one student for following the rules.

4 Designate a spot on the chalkboard as a scorekeeping area, or use a tracking chart. Throughout the day, as you spot different students being good, award a point with some words of praise:

"Jimmy has opened his book and has started reading. Good work, Jimmy, that's a point for the class toward the party on Friday."

How does this system specifically benefit your difficult students?

More motivation to choose appropriate behavior! If, for example, you have set a goal to give positive support to a specific student 10 times a day, turn those recognitions into classwide points and the positive effects will be doubled. The student receives praise and recognition from you, and the class moves closer to a reward, which earns recognition from them. The difficult student will be even more motivated to comply.

Also, by making sure that your difficult students are earning many of the classwide points you can really use this system as an individualized approach for recognizing these students.

Keep in mind also that your own words of recognition and praise when you award a point to a difficult student should be geared toward the student's primary need.

Here's how a classwide positive system will benefit each type of special need.

Students Who Need Attention

These students love attention, so they'll particularly like being a visible part of earning a reward the whole class wants. With a classwide motivation system, these students not only can earn attention from you but they get added attention from their peers. Every time they earn a point they'll help the class move ahead toward a reward.

Students Who Need Limits

These students may not want or even accept praise from you, but they may accept some adulation from the class. They may even enjoy the recognition and attention they get when they bring the class closer to it's reward—a hero! A classwide system gives the student an opportunity to choose appropriate behavior not for you, but for the class—a much more agreeable, perhaps powerful position. It puts the student in the leadership role—control role—that he or she wants. And the student is using appropriate behavior to do so.

Students Who Need Motivation

Having the whole class cheering them on can greatly boost their motivation to succeed. Whenever you see this child working, add a point to the board! The whole class will be appreciative and let the point-winning student know it.

Important: Earned points must never be taken away from the classwide tracking chart. Once a point is earned, it's "etched in stone." If students feel that the positives they worked so diligently for can be taken away, there will be no incentive to continue positive behavior.

Suggested Classwide Positive Reward Systems

Whatever the reward you offer, it should be something the entire class will participate in. This is the perfect opportunity to give the class a little break from their everyday classroom routine.

Classwide Positive Systems Page 80

Does your class enjoy music? Use the tracking chart on page 80. Make a check in a blank square each time you catch a student behaving appropriately. Be on the lookout for difficult students who are following the rules. When all of the blanks are checked off, the class earns a period of musical entertainment.

Tracking charts for pizza parties, movies and a game period are included on pages 80-81.

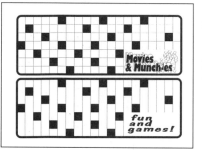

Classwide Positive Systems Page 81

Open-ended tracking charts can be found on page 82.

Here's another idea:

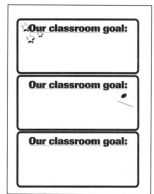

Goal Strips Page 83

Many middle-school and high-school students are motivated by goals related to academics. Here's something just for them:

On page 83 you will find a selection of Classroom Goal strips. Select a classwide goal your students will work toward. Write the goal on the strip and tape it on the chalkboard. Decide on the number of checks required for the class to earn the reward. Throughout the period, make marks on the chalkboard when individual students behave appropriately. Peer pressure and an attractive goal will get your class (and your difficult student) on the road to good behavior.

What's My P.S.Q.?
(Positive Support Quotient)

How positive are you with your difficult students? Place this tally sheet on a clipboard and carry it with you during the day or period. Write the names of your difficult students in the boxes. Keep track of the times a difficult student misbehaves and the times that you positively reinforce the student for choosing appropriate behavior. At the end of the day or period, tally up the marks. Your positives should equal or surpass the number of disruptions. Do they?

Name_____	Name_____	Name_____	Name_____
Misbehaviors	Misbehaviors	Misbehaviors	Misbehaviors
Total____	Total____	Total____	Total____
Positives	Positives	Positives	Positives
Total____	Total____	Total____	Total____

Name_____	Name_____	Name_____	Name_____
Misbehaviors	Misbehaviors	Misbehaviors	Misbehaviors
Total____	Total____	Total____	Total____
Positives	Positives	Positives	Positives
Total____	Total____	Total____	Total____

Name_____	Name_____	Name_____	Name_____
Misbehaviors	Misbehaviors	Misbehaviors	Misbehaviors
Total____	Total____	Total____	Total____
Positives	Positives	Positives	Positives
Total____	Total____	Total____	Total____

Name_____	Name_____	Name_____	Name_____
Misbehaviors	Misbehaviors	Misbehaviors	Misbehaviors
Total____	Total____	Total____	Total____
Positives	Positives	Positives	Positives
Total____	Total____	Total____	Total____

Positives Planner
Elementary

MONDAY

Name	Positives Goal	10		1	2	3	4	5	6	7	8	9	10
Name_____	Positives Goal	☐											
Name_____	Positives Goal	☐											
Name_____	Positives Goal	☐											
Name_____	Positives Goal	☐											

TUESDAY

Name_____	Positives Goal ☐
Name_____	Positives Goal ☐
Name_____	Positives Goal ☐
Name_____	Positives Goal ☐
Name_____	Positives Goal ☐

WEDNESDAY

Name_____	Positives Goal ☐
Name_____	Positives Goal ☐
Name_____	Positives Goal ☐
Name_____	Positives Goal ☐
Name_____	Positives Goal ☐

THURSDAY

Name_____	Positives Goal ☐
Name_____	Positives Goal ☐
Name_____	Positives Goal ☐
Name_____	Positives Goal ☐
Name_____	Positives Goal ☐

FRIDAY

Name_____	Positives Goal ☐
Name_____	Positives Goal ☐
Name_____	Positives Goal ☐
Name_____	Positives Goal ☐
Name_____	Positives Goal ☐

MONDAY

Period_____	Period_____	Period_____
Period_____	Period_____	Period_____

TUESDAY

Period_____	Period_____	Period_____
Period_____	Period_____	Period_____

WEDNESDAY

Period_____	Period_____	Period_____
Period_____	Period_____	Period_____

THURSDAY

Period_____	Period_____	Period_____
Period_____	Period_____	Period_____

FRIDAY

Period_____	Period_____	Period_____
Period_____	Period_____	Period_____

There's no time like the present to be POSITIVE!

Now's the time to be positive!

Look for Positives!

POSITIVE, POSITIVE, POSITIVE!

PLAN to be POSITIVE

One-to-One Praise

THUMBS UP!

Praise phrase begins with "YOU" instead of "I"

STUDENT FILE COPY

DATE:

Cue Card

for _____

STUDENT'S NAME

Providing Positive Support for the Student Who Needs Attention

Guidelines

At the elementary level, you can provide attention-seeking students positive attention openly and in front of their peers. Children at this age enjoy your "public" adulations. It gives them even more attention. And the added attention you give them with this open praise helps fulfill their need for attention.

Middle and secondary students still want your attention, but in consideration of their age and the effect of peer responses, you need to provide praise quietly and one-to-one.

For attention-seeking students of all ages:

- **Tie your praise to a specific behavior.**

Elementary:

"Michael, good job! Your group is doing fine work, and you're really helping."

Secondary:

(Quietly, while leaning down toward the student) "Excellent progress on this report, Sally. Keep it up!"

- **Give the praise immediately.**

N O T E S

Cue Card

for _____

STUDENT'S NAME

Providing Positive Support to the Student Who Needs Firmer Limits

Guidelines

The student who needs to be tough or in control does not want to receive your positive support in front of the entire class. Try these more subtle, one-to-one approaches instead.

For students of all ages:

- **Give verbal praise quietly and discreetly during or after class.**

- **Make eye contact and give a nod.**

- **Give a quick "thumbs up."**

- **Smile**

- **Write a note on the student's homework before you hand it back.**

- **Write a brief note to the student and quietly place it on his or her desk.**

Caution:

- **Be careful not to give praise too soon.**

- **Always approach the student in a low-keyed manner.**

- **The younger the student, the more explicit you can be in your praise.**

  "Jason, good job entering the classroom."

- **Be less explicit and more casual and general with older students.**

  "Miranda, keep it up."

- **Be wary of touching the student or making any other kind of physical contact.**

- **Make "you" statements rather than "I" statements. These students are not working to please *you*.**

  No– *"I like the way you've started to read.*

  Yes– Simply nod and quietly say, *"Your book is open and you're reading. Alright!"*

N O T E S

_____
_____
_____
_____
_____
_____
_____
_____
_____
_____
_____
_____
_____
_____
_____
_____
_____

STUDENT FILE COPY

STUDENT FILE COPY

DATE:

Cue Card

for _____

Providing Positive Support to the Student Who Needs Motivation

Guidelines

Always connect your positive support to the student's academic efforts. These students need constant encouragement to keep their enthusiasm high. Approach the student one-to-one and let him or her know that you applaud the work accomplished and that you have confidence that he or she can continue to do well.

For students of all ages:

- **Tie your praise to academic efforts.**

  "Sarah, you've completed half the problems on the page. Excellent!"

- **Give the praise immediately.**

- **Praise students individually and quietly.**

N O T E S

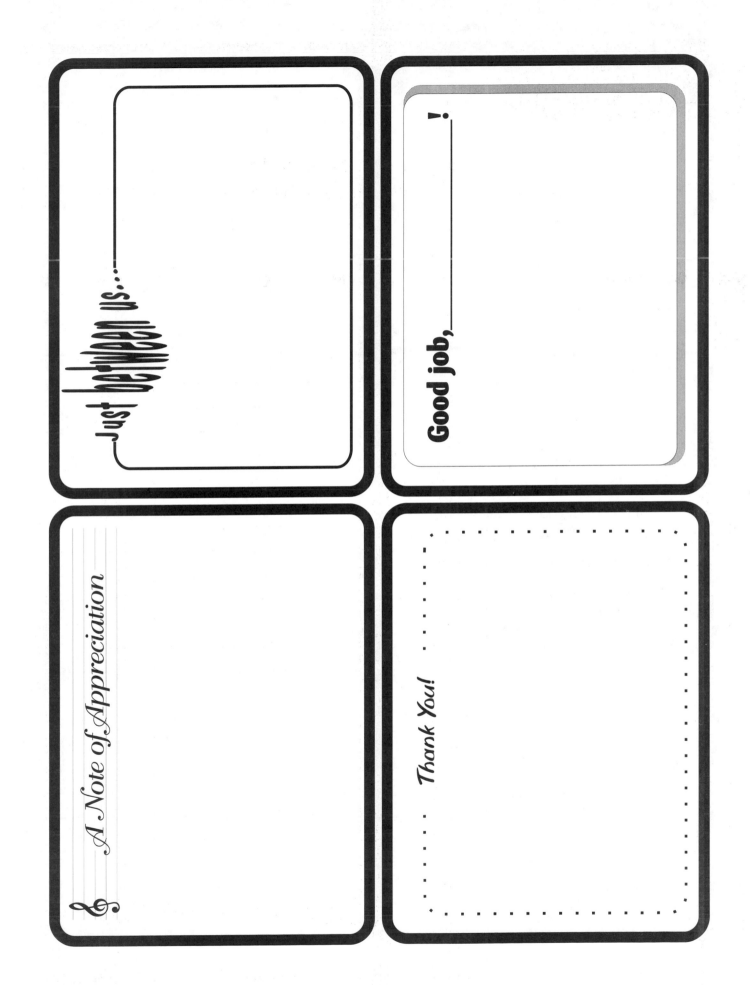

Just between us....

Good job, _____!

A Note of Appreciation

Thank You!

Something to share

To: _____

_____

_____

_____

_____

_____

Teacher's Signature

Something to share

To: _____

_____

_____

_____

_____

_____

_____

Teacher's Signature

Something to share

To: _____

_____

_____

_____

_____

_____

Teacher's Signature

Positive Phone Call
Planning Sheet

Date_____

Student's Name_____Phone #_____

Reason for call _____

_____

_____

Student comments _____

_____

Positive Phone Call
Planning Sheet

Date_____

Student's Name_____Phone #_____

Reason for call _____

_____

_____

Student comments _____

_____

Positive Phone Call
Planning Sheet

Date_____

Student's Name_____Phone #_____

Reason for call _____

_____

_____

Student comments _____

_____

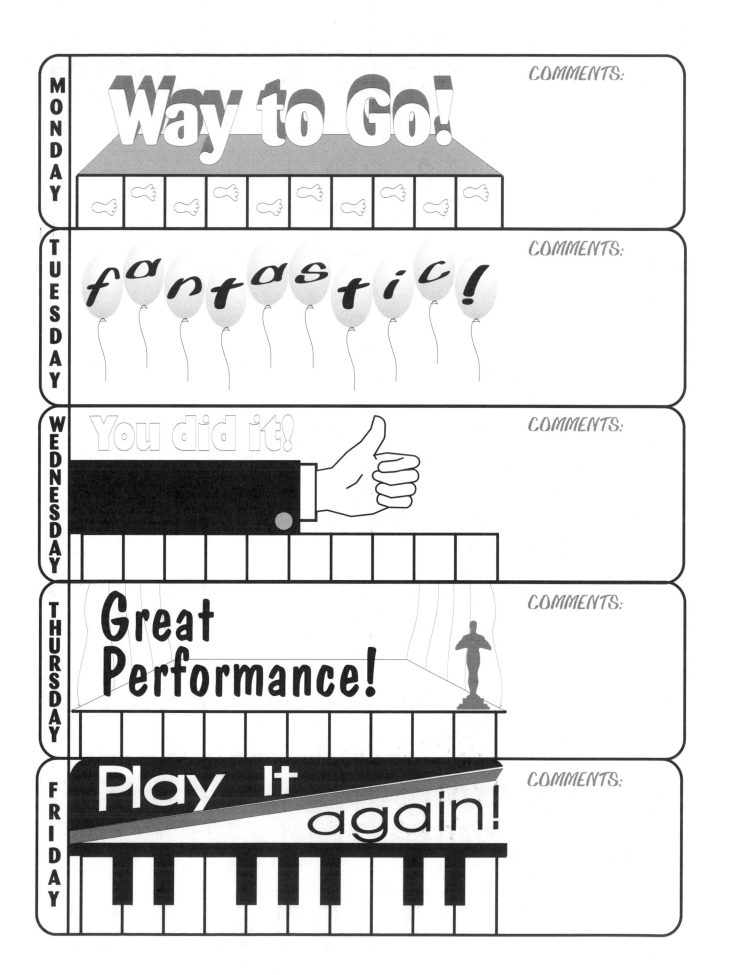

MONDAY

Way to Go!

COMMENTS:

TUESDAY

fantastic!

COMMENTS:

WEDNESDAY

You did it!

COMMENTS:

THURSDAY

Great Performance!

COMMENTS:

FRIDAY

Play It again!

COMMENTS:

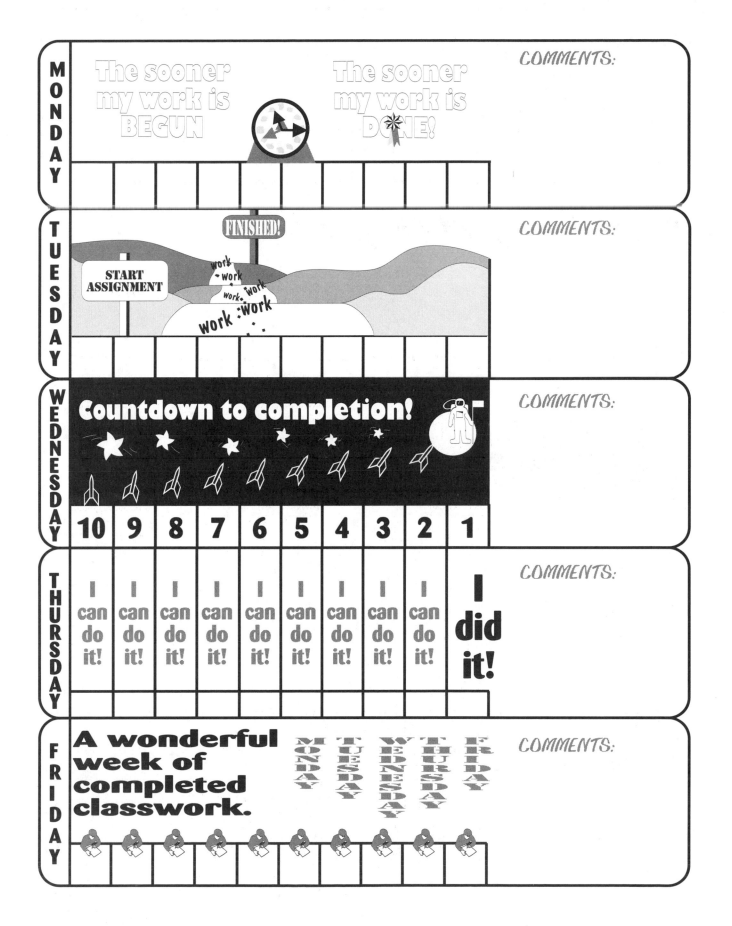

MONDAY

The sooner my work is BEGUN   The sooner my work is DONE!

COMMENTS:

TUESDAY

FINISHED!

START ASSIGNMENT

work • work • work • work work • work work :work

COMMENTS:

WEDNESDAY

Countdown to completion!

10	9	8	7	6	5	4	3	2	1

COMMENTS:

THURSDAY

I can do it!	I can do it!	I can do it!	I can do it!	I can do it!	I can do it!	I can do it!	I can do it!	I can do it!	I did it!

COMMENTS:

FRIDAY

A wonderful week of completed classwork.

MONDAY TUESDAY WEDNESDAY THURSDAY FRIDAY

COMMENTS:

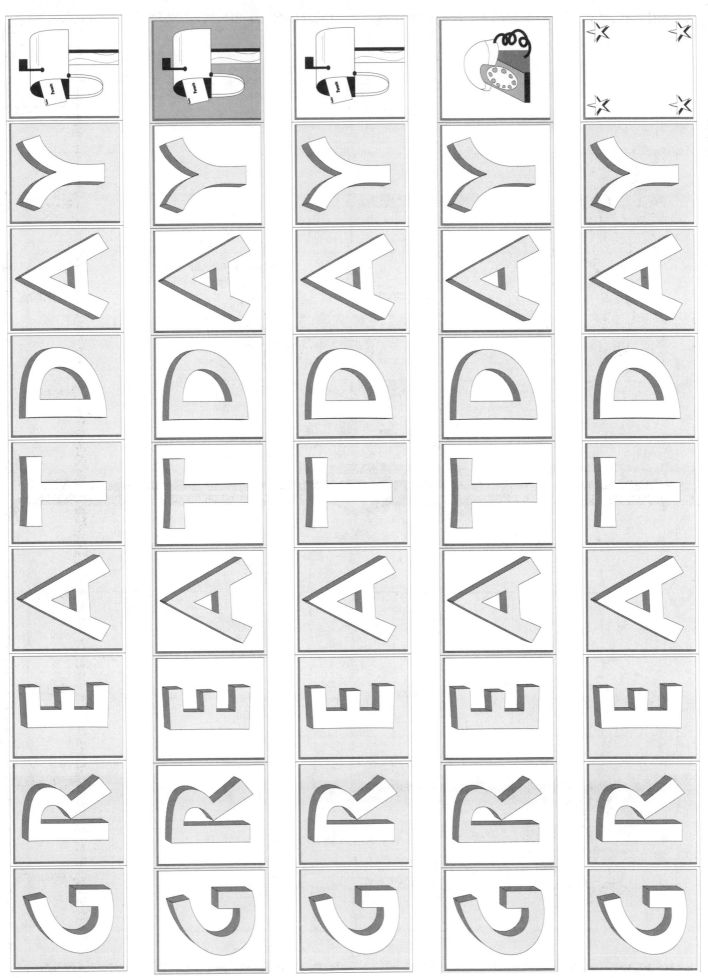

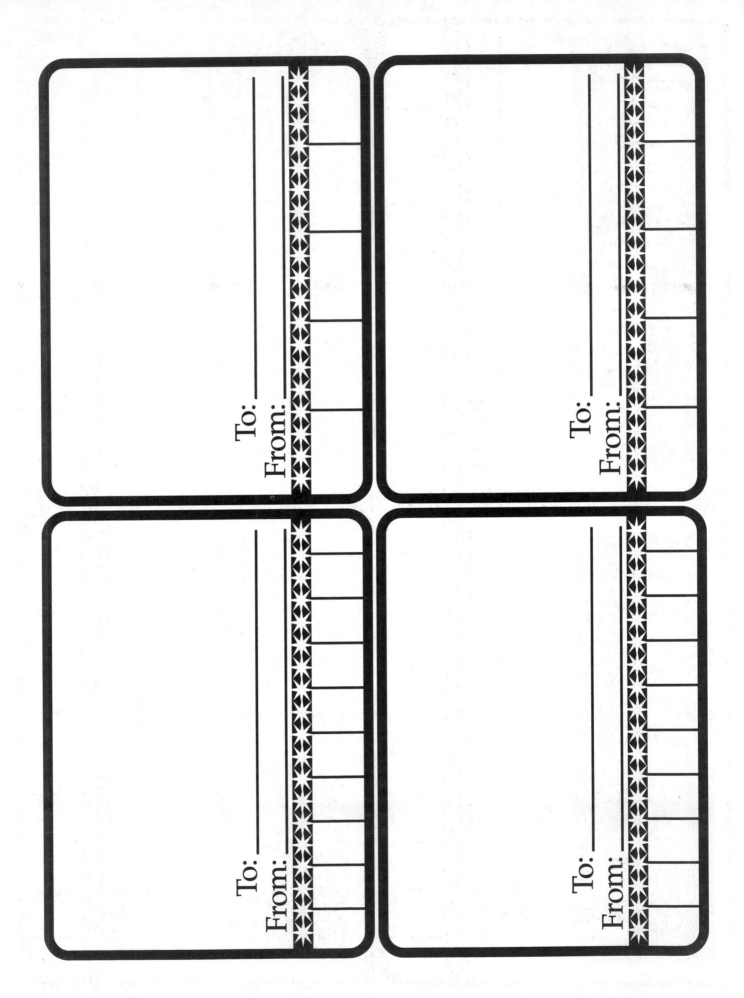

To:

From:

To:

From:

To:

From:

To:

From:

NO HOMEWORK COUPON

To: _____

From: _____

CHANGE SEAT COUPON

To: _____

From: _____

FREE LUNCH COUPON

To: _____

From: _____

FREE DRINK COUPON

To: _____

From: _____

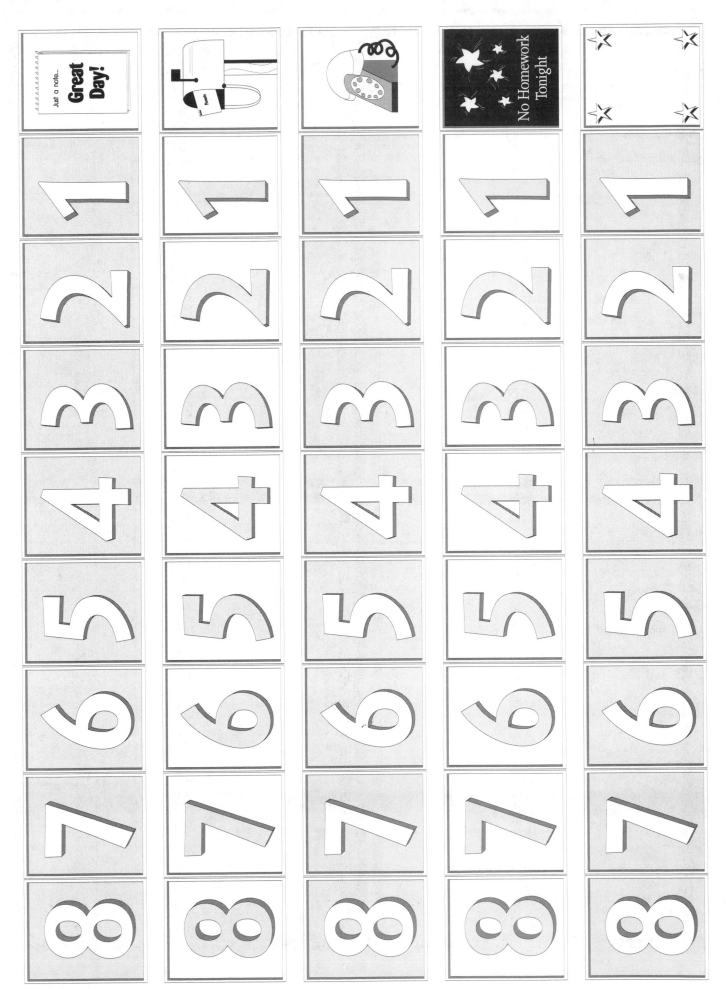

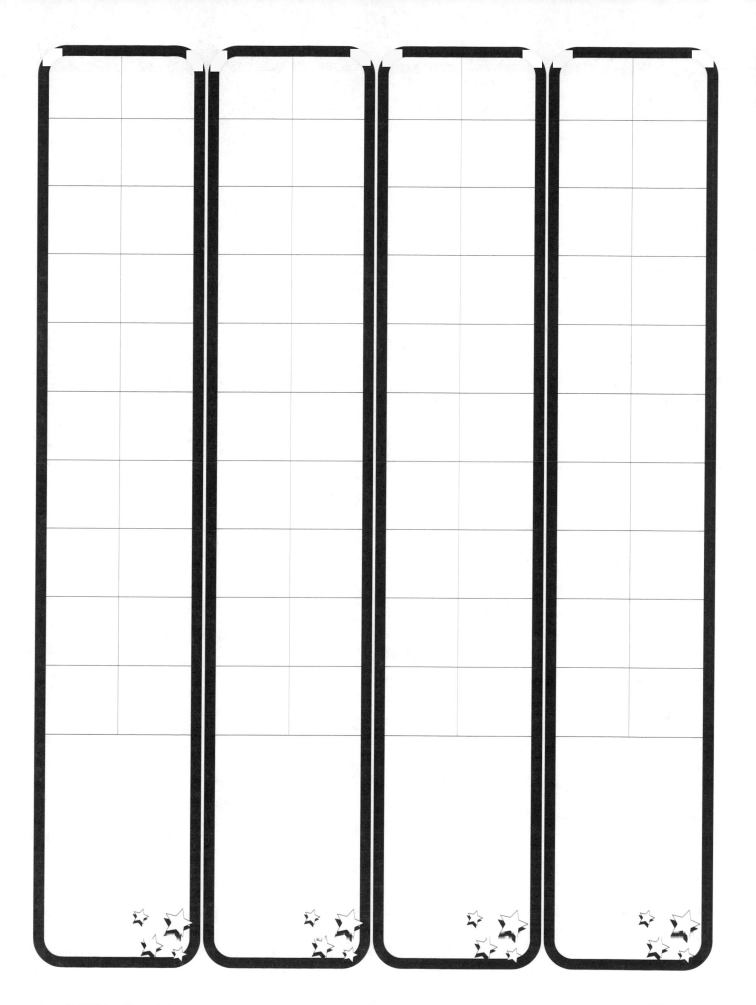

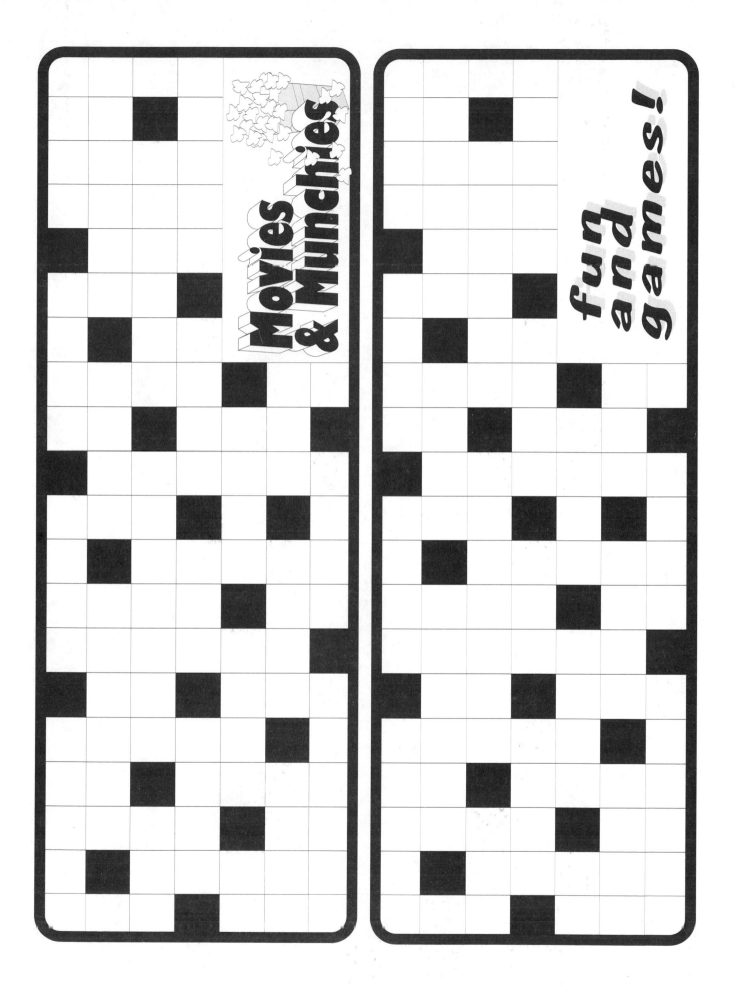

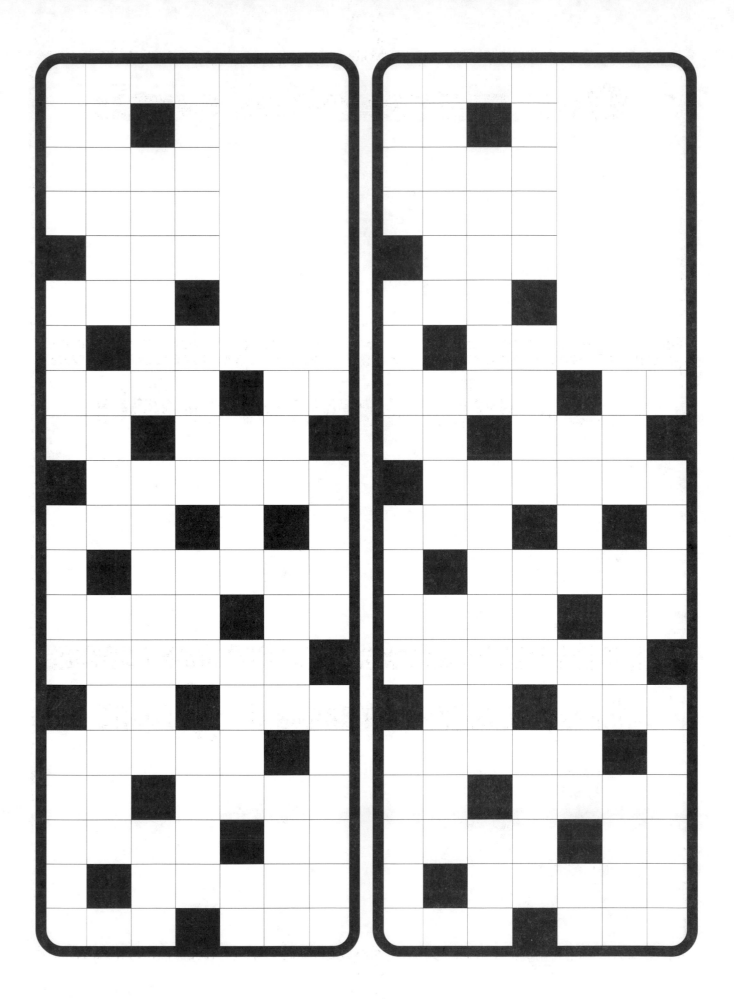

⭐ Our classroom goal:

Our classroom goal:

Our classroom goal:

Student File Update

STUDENT FILE COPY

At this point your Student File should contain the following:

- ☑ Phone Call Record Sheet
- ☑ Relationship-Building Plan
- ☑ Student Interest Inventory
- ☑ 15+ Ways to Develop Positive Relationships with Students
- ☑ Primary Need Worksheet
- ☑ Goals Sheet
- ☑ Behavior Profile
- ☑ Lesson Plan(s) for Teaching Appropriate Behavior
- ☑ Providing Positive Support Cue Card
- ☑ Positive Phone Call Planner
- ☐ Redirecting Technique Cue Card

- ☐ Cue Card for Providing Consequences
- ☐ Cue Card for Defusing Covert Confrontations
- ☐ Cue Card for Defusing Overt Confrontations
- ☐ Cue Card for Conducting a Problem-Solving Conference
- ☐ Problem-Solving Conference Worksheet
- ☐ Any documentation pertaining to an Individualized Behavior Plan you are using with the student.
- ☐ Substitute's Plan

Reminders

- Prompt reinforcement is effective reinforcement.

Be sure to give positive recognition immediately after you have observed the desired behavior. You want the student to associate this behavior with the reward, and the longer you wait, the less effective the reinforcer will be.

- Pair positives with praise.

Whenever you give a student a tangible reward, a special privilege or a behavior award, always pair it with specific praise such as "Here's a coupon for working so well with your group today, Gabe."

Your Next Step ▶▶▶

You've been given ideas and techniques for reinforcing appropriate behavior. Now, what do you do when your difficult student chooses to continue inappropriate behavior?

Part 5

Redirect Nondisruptive Off-Task Behavior

Consistent positive recognition of your student's appropriate behavior will increase the likelihood of that behavior continuing. But you're probably familiar enough with difficult students to know that there still will be times when they will behave inappropriately.

If you plan ahead how you will respond to the misbehavior you will be able to stay in control and handle the situation with confidence.

There are two types of inappropriate classroom behavior that hinder a student's success in school: disruptive behavior and nondisruptive off-task behavior.

Disruptive behavior is behavior that keeps you from teaching and keeps other students from learning. Disruptive behaviors include talking back, arguing, tantrums, fighting, making noises or openly refusing to work.

Nondisruptive off-task behavior is behavior that is off task but is not disturbing others. These behaviors include staring out the window, not doing assigned work, doodling, putting head down on desk. The student isn't doing anything to bother you or anyone else, but he or she isn't learning or participating either.

The nondisruptive off-task behavior of a difficult student is often handled in one of two ways by the teacher—it is either ignored or immediately punished. Neither of these responses is in the student's best interest.

- Ignoring the behavior tells the student that it doesn't matter to you whether or not he or she is a part of the class, and this is the last thing a difficult student needs to feel.

- Providing an immediate consequence when a lesser response might suffice will only further alienate an already troubled, alienated student.

The best response to nondisruptive off-task behavior is to first try to redirect the student back on task.

Redirecting techniques are subtle cues you can use that will let the student know he or she needs to get back to work. They are not punitive or embarrassing. Rather, they are a helpful nudge that will give the student an opportunity to make a better choice.

On the following pages you will find specific redirecting techniques for students who need attention and students who need firmer limits.

Note: Redirecting techniques in and of themselves are generally not effective with students who need motivation. These students need massive amounts of motivation and encouragement. Redirecting techniques, therefore, are often too subtle to be of value.

For easy access, the redirecting techniques have been organized on Cue Cards (pages 87-88).

Reproduce the card that pertains to your own student, review the information and add it to his or her file. Whenever you need to refresh yourself on these techniques, the information will be easy to find. Use the "Notes" section of the Cue Card to record any comments you may want to add pertaining to the use of these techniques with your student.

CueCard
Redirecting Techniques for the Student Who Needs Attention, Page 87
Firmer Limits, Page 88

Cue Card
for _____
STUDENT'S NAME

Redirecting Techniques for the Student Who Needs Attention

The student who needs attention is usually the easiest to redirect back on task. After all, this student *wants* your attention. By giving that attention in a redirecting manner you'll be meeting his or her needs and positively guiding the student toward better behavior choices at the same time.

These techniques are effective with the student who needs attention:

The Look

When a student stares off into space or gazes out the window, just catch his or her eye and give a look—a purposeful, meaningful look that says, "I've noticed your behavior, I disapprove, and I want you to get back on task now!"

Then hold that look until the student gets back on task.

Physical Proximity

When you notice that a student has fallen off task, just walk over and stand by his or her desk. You may tap the student on the shoulder, or you may just stand there. Either way, the message (and your attention) is communicated.

Mention the Student's Name

When a student is falling off task, simply wake him or her up a bit by including the student's name in your lesson. Ask the student for an answer to a question or to work a problem on the board. Be sure to positively reinforce the student once he or she is back on task.

N O T E S

DATE:

STUDENT NAME:

CLASS/PERIOD:

Cue Card

for _____
STUDENT'S NAME

Redirecting Techniques for the Student Who Needs Firmer Limits

The confrontational student—that student who needs firmer limits—absolutely does not want your attention. Redirecting techniques, therefore, must be delivered quietly without drawing a lot of attention to the student.

These techniques are effective with the student who needs firmer limits:

Seat the Student by You

Many teachers seat their confrontational students as far away from them as possible, but the closer this difficult student is seated to you, the easier it will be for you to guide him or her toward better behavioral choices and build a positive relationship with the student. When the student is close to you, your interactions can be more discreet, less obvious to the rest of the students. This allows your student to save face, which lessens resistance to you and your efforts.

Physical Proximity

Standing by a student who needs firm limits may be sufficient to motivate him or her back on task. By proactively planning to be there, you can deter this student's tendency to go off task. You can stay on top of the situation and nip inappropriate behavior in the bud.

Remind the Student about the Rules

Reminding a student of the directions he or she is to follow is an excellent technique to use with a student who needs limits.

In a low-key manner, simply state your behavioral expectations:

> "Remember, Elise, take your books, walk straight to your social studies group and sit down without talking."

This message can be delivered without drawing attention to the student—but the student will get the message loud and clear.

NOTES

Student File Update

STUDENT FILE COPY

At this point your Student File should contain the following:

☑ Phone Call Record Sheet

☑ Relationship-Building Plan

☑ Student Interest Inventory

☑ 15+ Ways to Develop Positive Relationships with Students

☑ Primary Need Worksheet

☑ Goals Sheet

☑ Behavior Profile

☑ Lesson Plan(s) for Teaching Appropriate Behavior

☑ Providing Positive Support Cue Card

☑ Positive Phone Call Planner

☑ Redirecting Technique Cue Card

☐ Cue Card for Providing Consequences

☐ Cue Card for Defusing Covert Confrontations

☐ Cue Card for Defusing Overt Confrontations

☐ Cue Card for Conducting a Problem-Solving Conference

☐ Problem-Solving Conference Worksheet

☐ Any documentation pertaining to an Individualized Behavior Plan you are using with the student.

☐ Substitute's Plan

Reminders

- Once the student is redirected back on task, don't just let it go at that. Give plenty of positive reinforcement for the behavior choice the student has made. As always, provide the positive support in a manner that fits the student's needs.

- With difficult students, nondisruptive off-task behavior is often a precursor to more disruptive behavior. By redirecting the behavior you will lessen the likelihood of it escalating and therefore lessen the likelihood of having to turn to more substantial responses.

Your Next Step ▶ ▶ ▶

The next section of this workbook will address how to respond to disruptive behavior.

Part 6
Decreasing Disruptive Behavior

When your difficult student chooses to disrupt—when he or she stops you from teaching and other students from learning—you'll have to be prepared to use corrective actions, or consequences, to get the student back on task.

Difficult students must be held accountable to the same behavioral limits as your other students. The student's eventual success will depend upon a balance between the positive relationship you are building by reaching out to him or her and the limits you set and enforce.

- The goal of the consequences you give a difficult student should be to stop the unacceptable behavior and to help the student make better choices or learn a new behavior. *Consequences are not meant to punish a student.*

- It is not the severity of the consequence that matters. It is the consistency with which it is implemented. Difficult students require more structure than other students. They must absolutely understand that every time they choose to disrupt, you will intervene and take action. Minimal consequences are often the most effective because you are likely to use them consistently.

- When appropriate, the consequence should be given immediately or as soon as possible after the disruption. Your goal is to teach acceptable behavior. A consequence given hours after the fact will not be as effective as one that can be provided sooner.

Discipline Hierarchy

Many teachers use consequences within the context of a discipline hierarchy that is part of a general classroom discipline plan.

A classroom discipline plan is a behavior management system that allows you to spell out the behavior you expect from all students and what they can expect from you in return. This plan provides an extremely effective framework around which all of your classroom management efforts can be organized.

A classroom discipline plan consists of three parts:

Rules that all students must follow at all times.

Positive Recognition that students will receive for following the rules.

Consequences that result when students choose not to follow the rules.

A well-defined classroom discipline plan is the foundation of a smoothly running, effective and motivating classroom. Teachers often find that having such a plan in place can greatly minimize disruptive behavior in their classrooms.

Sample Classroom Discipline Plan (Middle School)

Classroom Rules

Follow directions.
Keep hands, feet and objects to yourself.
No swearing, teasing or name calling.

Positive Recognition

Praise
Positive notes sent home to parents
Select own seat for the day

Consequences (Discipline Hierarchy)

First time student breaks a rule:	Warning
Second time:	Stay in class 1 minute after the bell.
Third time:	Stay in class 2 minutes after the bell.
Fourth time:	Teacher calls parents.
Fifth time:	Send to principal.

Severe Clause (for major infraction):

Send to principal.

Using a Discipline Hierarchy as Part of a Classroom Plan

A discipline hierarchy lists consequences in the order in which they will be imposed for noncompliant behavior (breaking classroom rules) within a day or within a class period. The hierarchy is progressive, starting with a warning the first time a student breaks a rule. The consequences then become gradually more substantial for the second, third, fourth and fifth time that a student disrupts in a day or class period.

For example, take a look at the sample discipline hierarchy for grades 4-6 below.

First time a student breaks a rule:	Warning
Second time:	10 minutes working away from the group
Third time:	15 minutes working away from the group
Fourth time:	Call parents
Fifth time:	Send to principal
Major Infraction: (Severe Clause)	Send immediately to principal

A finite set of consequences such as this is important for a well-managed classroom. The students will understand exactly what will happen each time they misbehave. This gives them a sense of security in understanding the parameters of how the teacher will respond. This hierarchy of consequences also gives the teacher a sense of security because he or she knows how to respond to misbehavior without worrying about being unfair or reactive.

If you already have a discipline hierarchy in place as part of a classroom discipline plan, stop and evaluate it. If you have a large number of difficult students you may choose to either change the consequences (see suggested consequences on pages 96-98) or individualize the way you provide the consequences (see the Cue Cards on pages 100-102).

When evaluating your consequences, ask yourself:

- Are the consequences so inconvenient to impose that I am not giving them consistently?

- Are the consequences not enough of a deterrent to matter to my students?

- Are the consequences so severe that my students react with increased anger and hostility?

If you do not have a discipline hierarchy in place:

Here are guidelines for developing a discipline hierarchy. Although you can create a hierarchy for a single student, ideally it should be in place for the entire class as part of a fully developed classroom discipline plan. It demonstrates to your difficult students that they are accountable to the same expectations as are other students.

• First Time a Student Disrupts

Most teachers issue a warning the first time a student disrupts or breaks a rule of the classroom.

> "Corey, the direction was to work without talking. That's a warning."

> "Gary, the rule in this classroom is no swearing. That's a warning."

A warning gives the student an opportunity to choose more appropriate behavior before a more substantial consequence is received. It is a powerful reminder, one that carries an important message. The student knows that the next disruption will bring with it a real consequence.

• Second Time a Student Disrupts

The second or third time a student disrupts in the same day, or the same period, the teacher needs to provide a consequence. These consequences must be easy to implement, and not time consuming. Typical consequences for second or third infractions include time out, one-minute wait after class, and filling out a Think Sheet. (The Think Sheet is explained on pages 96-97.)

• Fourth Time a Student Disrupts

You need to contact parents if a student disrupts a fourth time in a day (self-contained classrooms) or in a class period (upper grades).

Parent contact is a key component of managing student behavior. For some students, involving parents will be the only way you will motivate them toward appropriate behavior. Teachers typically give the parent a call or send a note home to let the parent know that a student's behavior is disruptive and cannot continue. Students need to know that you will be consistent in the enforcement of this consequence. And parents need to know where they fit in.

• Fifth Time a Student Disrupts

Sending a student to the principal or vice principal should be the last consequence on a discipline hierarchy. In preparation for implementing this consequence, you must have already met with your administrator to discuss actions he or she will take when students are sent to the office. You need to know that the administrator will provide the help and support you need. The administrator's role might include counseling with the student, conferencing with the parents or suspending a severely disruptive student.

• Severe Clause

In cases of severe misbehavior, such as fighting, vandalism, defying a teacher or in some way stopping the entire class from functioning, a student would not receive a warning. He or she loses the right to proceed through the hierarchy of consequences. Severe misbehavior calls for an immediate consequence that will remove the student from the classroom.

On a discipline hierarchy this is called a Severe Clause.

Sample Discipline Hierarchy for Grades K-3

First time a student breaks a rule:	Warning
Second time:	5 minutes working away from the group
Third time:	10 minutes working away from the group
Fourth time:	Call parents
Fifth time:	Send to principal
Severe Clause:	Send to principal

Sample Discipline Hierarchy for Grades 4-6

First time a student breaks a rule:	Warning
Second time:	10 minutes working away from the group
Third time:	15 minutes working away from the group plus fill out a Think Sheet
Fourth time:	Call parents
Fifth time:	Send to principal
Severe Clause:	Send to principal

Sample Discipline Hierarchy for Grades 7-12

First time student breaks a rule:	Warning
Second time:	Stay in class 1 minute after the bell
Third time:	Stay in class 2 minutes after the bell plus fill out a Think Sheet
Fourth time:	Call parents
Fifth time:	Send to administrator
Severe Clause:	Send to administrator

A discipline hierarchy is a very effective way to use consequences with all of your students. The value of a hierarchy is that everyone—you, students and parents—will know exactly what will happen each time misbehavior occurs. No surprises. No unequal treatment.

> For complete guidelines for developing and implementing a discipline hierarchy as part of a complete classroom discipline plan, please see Lee Canter's revised *Assertive Discipline— Positive Behavior Management for Today's Classroom.*

Suggested Consequences

On the following pages you will find a selection of consequences that teachers have proven effective in their classrooms.

- Time Out
- Have Student Call Parent
- Think Sheet
  (in conjunction with another corrective action)

- One Minute After Class
- Write Letter Home

Time Out

One of the most effective corrective interventions for elementary students is to simply remove the student from the situation in which he or she is disrupting. During this time out, the student sits apart from the rest of the class, but is expected to continue to do work or listen to the lesson. If appropriate, a very disruptive difficult student can be seated close to you so you can easily monitor his or her behavior, give positive feedback or redirect behavior as needed.

The advantages to time out are twofold:

1 By removing the student from the situation in which he or she is disrupting, you immediately stop the disruptive behavior. The rest of the class can get back on task.

2 The student is given an opportunity to calm down and get back on task without the distraction of other students.

Think Sheet

Your goal in providing a consequence is not to punish, but to stop this misbehavior and keep it from escalating. A Think Sheet provides an excellent opportunity for an older student to stop and evaluate his or her inappropriate behavior and also to consider other behaviors that might be better choices in the future.

If age appropriate, when a student is disruptive, or breaks a classroom rule, have him or her write an account of the misbehavior during recess, after class or at home.

The Think Sheet should include the following points:

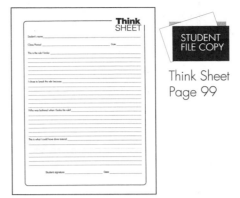

STUDENT FILE COPY

Think Sheet
Page 99

- The misbehavior or rule that was broken

- Why the student chose to misbehave

- Who was bothered (fellow students, teacher, etc.)

- What more appropriate behavior the student could choose next time

The Think Sheet gives the student an opportunity to calmly think through his or her behavioral choices. The Think Sheet will also provide you a "student's point of view" forum from which to address a student's problem behavior in a one-to-one conference. We'll look further into this in Part 7.

Note: The Think Sheet in and of itself is not a consequence, but should be given in conjunction with another corrective action such as time out or detention. The act of filling out the Think Sheet helps to calm the student down and evaluate his or her behavior.

One Minute After Class

For middle or secondary students, one of the most effective corrective interventions is to keep the student after class for one minute.

Remember, it isn't the severity of a consequence, it is the consistency with which it is used that makes it effective.

To an older student, one minute away from peers, away from the group, can seem like forever. Just one minute is enough to make a student miss walking to the next class with friends, be last in line at lunch or miss joining a group after school. Don't underestimate the power of this consequence for older students.

In this one minute, you also have an opportunity to briefly speak with the student about his or her behavior, work on the relationship and help the student make better behavior choices in the future.

And the ease of use of this consequence increases the likelihood that you will be consistent in its use.

Have Student Call Parent

Requiring a student to explain his or her disruptive behavior to a parent can be an extremely strong deterrent.

Some teachers today have portable telephones in their classroom and have had great success in having a student call his or her parent immediately after the student has been disruptive. This phone call could take place at recess, at lunch or at the end of the period. Having a phone available and calling immediately communicates to the student that you are serious about setting limits.

If a phone is not available in your classroom, the student needs to call as soon as both of you can get to a phone in the building.

Have Student Write a Letter Home

Writing a letter home explaining misbehavior can also be an effective consequence, particularly for older students. In the letter, the student simply explains to the parent how he or she misbehaved. Caution: Do not use this consequence if you have suspicions that a parent might respond with hostility and harm the child.

Major Infractions

No matter what system you use for delivering consequences, you must have a plan in place for dealing with severe misbehavior.

Sometimes you have to act quickly and decisively to stop a student's disruptive behavior. In cases of severe misbehavior, such as fighting, vandalism, defying a teacher or in some way stopping the entire class from functioning, a student must be removed immediately from the classroom.

Talk to your administrator about how major infractions will be dealt with and what support you can expect. Many schools have "Discipline Squads" consisting of two or three staff members who can be sent to a classroom to help remove a highly disruptive student.

Just as it is important to give positive recognition in a manner that will be most effectively received by the difficult student, it is also important to individualize the manner in which you give consequences.

The Cue Cards on pages 100-102 give guidelines for providing consequences to students who need attention, students who need firmer limits and students who need motivation. Reproduce the Cue Card that applies to your student. Keep it available for reference in the student's file. Use the "Notes" section to record any documentation you might want to keep concerning the use of these techniques with your student.

CueCard
Providing Consequences to the Student Who Needs Attention, Page 100
Firmer Limits, Page 101
Motivation, Page 102

Think
SHEET

Student's name_____

Class/Period _____ Date _____

This is the rule I broke: _____

_____

_____

_____

_____

_____

_____

I chose to break this rule because: _____

_____

_____

_____

_____

_____

_____

Who was bothered when I broke this rule? _____

_____

_____

_____

_____

_____

This is what I could have done instead: _____

_____

_____

_____

_____

_____

Student signature _____ Date _____

STUDENT FILE COPY

DATE:

Cue Card

for _____
STUDENT'S NAME

Providing Consequences to the Student Who Needs Attention

Your number-one goal when providing consequences to a student who needs attention is to give the *minimal* amount of attention you possibly can.

The reason the student may have been disruptive in the first place was to gain attention. Don't reward inappropriate behavior.

When giving the consequence be as brief as possible. You may want to just write the student's name on your clipboard and simply say, "Doug, the direction was to work without talking. That's a warning." No discussion. No attention.

If the disruptive behavior continues, keep your responses brief and to the point. "Doug, that's a check—one minute after class."

Don't perseverate on the issue. Continue with your lesson. The student needs to learn that he or she will not get attention for misbehavior.

N O T E S

Cue Card

for _____

Providing Consequences to the Student Who Needs Firmer Limits

Stay very calm. If you're confrontational or very public when giving a consequence to this student, you're only going to get more confrontation in return and open the door to even more disruption as the student attempts to save face.

Don't raise your voice, and don't get upset. Speak quietly and avoid embarrassing the student. Walk over to the student and give him or her a choice to either comply with directions or choose the corrective action.

For example:

A seventh-grade teacher has given a direction to get started on an assignment. One student, Kevin, has paid no attention to the direction and begins to draw pictures on his binder. The teacher walks over to Kevin's desk, leans down and speaks calmly to him.

Teacher: *(in a soft voice) Kevin, the directions are to take your notebook and a pencil out and begin working on the assignment. You have a choice. You can follow these directions or you can wait one minute after class. The choice is yours, Kevin.*

Note: Give the student some time to respond. You must give limit-seeking students adequate time to save face. Let them huff. Let them puff. Let them go into slow motion. They need to do it. If they comply within fifteen seconds, you've achieved your goal. The student has chosen appropriate behavior.

Fifteen seconds, however, is long enough to wait. If a student doesn't comply within that amount of time then he or she probably isn't going to comply at all.

N O T E S

_____
_____
_____
_____
_____
_____
_____
_____
_____
_____
_____
_____
_____
_____
_____
_____
_____
_____
_____
_____
_____
_____

STUDENT FILE COPY

DATE:

Cue Card

for _____

STUDENT'S NAME

Providing Consequences to the Student Who Needs Motivation

Unless the student is overtly disruptive or refuses to do work, the only action that must be taken with a student who needs motivation is that he or she is required to finish the assigned amount of work. The student must recognize that you are not going away. If the work is not finished in class, the student will need to finish it at another time, whether at recess, lunch, after school, or at home.

For example:

- **You will finish incomplete assignments at recess, lunch or before school.**

- **You will finish incomplete assignments during before-school detention or during after-school detention.**

A sixth-grade class is working on an assignment. Gerrie, a student who needs motivation, is sitting at her desk staring at her paper, but making no attempt to do the work. Her teacher walks over to her.

"Gerrie, I expect you to do this assignment today. You have a choice. You can finish it now, in class, or you can come back to the room after you eat and finish it then. It's up to you, Gerrie."

N O T E S

STUDENT FILE COPY | Student File Update

At this point your Student File should contain the following:

- ☑ Phone Call Record Sheet
- ☑ Relationship-Building Plan
- ☑ Student Interest Inventory
- ☑ 15+ Ways to Develop Positive Relationships with Students
- ☑ Primary Need Worksheet
- ☑ Goals Sheet
- ☑ Behavior Profile
- ☑ Lesson Plan(s) for Teaching Appropriate Behavior
- ☑ Providing Positive Support Cue Card
- ☑ Positive Phone Call Planner
- ☑ Redirecting Technique Cue Card

- ☑ Cue Card for Providing Consequences
- ☐ Cue Card for Defusing Covert Confrontations
- ☐ Cue Card for Defusing Overt Confrontations
- ☐ Cue Card for Conducting a Problem-Solving Conference
- ☐ Problem-Solving Conference Worksheet
- ☐ Any documentation pertaining to an Individualized Behavior Plan you are using with the student.
- ☐ Substitute's Plan

Reminders

- Consequences are not an end in and of themselves, but a part of the relationship-building process. They are designed to teach, not punish. If you use consequences to "get" kids, you won't get anywhere. Most difficult students have had enough neglect, abuse, anger and disapproval. What they have not had enough of is a positive relationship with their teacher.

- Consequences are not the only behavior management effort you are making with this student. Day in and day out you're always working on creating a positive relationship built on trust and high expectations. Any corrective actions you take must go hand in hand with your ongoing objective of maintaining this positive relationship.

- With difficult students, there can be no inconsistency. They need structure— clearly defined behavioral parameters. Students need to know that consequences are real results of choices they make. Inconsistency only reinforces their mistaken belief that they can do what they choose to do, and it's only by chance or bad luck that anything negative will come of it at all.

Your Next Step

Communicating effectively with a difficult student, especially in tough situations, requires special skills. These skills are the focus of the next section of this workbook.

Part 7

Communicating with Difficult Students

Difficult students will argue, be confrontational, critical, angry, verbally abusive, sullen and rude. When all of this negativity is aimed at you it's easy to react emotionally and respond with anger or irritation.

These responses will not build trust or enhance your relationship with the student, nor will they help the student to comply.

Communicating with a difficult student requires planning and skills. You need to know how to avoid reactive responses and refocus your energies on helping the student make better behavioral choices.

Confrontations with difficult students are inevitable. However, as the student continues to build trust in you and a positive relationship develops, these confrontations will become less frequent and less difficult. But don't expect overnight changes. For some students, change may come very slowly. For others change may not come at all while you are the student's teacher. Keep the big picture in mind. Do not let confrontations shake your resolve to make a difference with this student. Instead, view the confrontation as another opportunity to drive home to the student the fact that you are committed to helping him or her succeed.

In this section of the workbook you will learn techniques for defusing confrontations and conducting one-to-one problem-solving conferences.

Defusing Confrontations

When you set limits and hold difficult students accountable there will be confrontations. If you are to help the student through the confrontation and help yourself avoid unnecessary stress and anxiety, you need to be prepared to deal with these situations in a calm, proactive manner.

Confrontations with students take two different forms: covert and overt.

A **covert** confrontation occurs when a student responds to you with a sneer, a dirty look, mumbles under his or her breath or does something hostile that others in the class are unaware of.

An **overt** confrontation occurs when a student blatantly comes after you and the whole class is aware of it. The student may verbally defy your authority, be insulting or talk back.

The next two Cue Cards (pages 108-109) give you guidelines for handling each type of confrontation. Keep these Cue Cards in your student's file. Review them periodically so you will be prepared to respond effectively rather than reactively. Use the "Notes" section of the cards to record comments concerning your use of these techniques with your student.

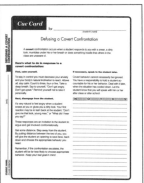

CueCard

Defusing a Covert Confrontation Page 108

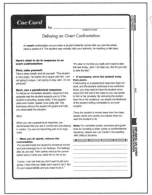

CueCard

Defusing an Overt Confrontation Page 109

One-to-One Problem Solving

If your student continues to have behavior problems, providing a consequence may stop the misbehavior for the moment, but by itself it will not help the student learn to make better choices in the future.

When misbehavior continues, your student needs to receive more in-depth and personal guidance from you. You need to sit down in a one-to-one problem-solving conference, listen to the student's concerns, firmly clarify your own expectations, and then work together to arrive at a practical course of action.

The goal of this meeting is not to punish, but to provide caring and guidance to a student who needs both. It's a chance to listen, to find out what your student is feeling and thinking, and a chance to build your relationship. The overall tone of the meeting should be a message of both commitment and of firmness.

When should you meet with your student in a one-to-one problem-solving conference?

Here are some guidelines:

- **Meet with a student in a one-to-one problem-solving conference when inappropriate behavior is chronic.**

    If misbehavior continues in spite of all the efforts you have made, it is time to work with the student to both clarify your expectations and structure some alternative actions the student can take.

- **Meet with a student in a one-to-one problem-solving conference when there is a sudden behavior change.**

    If a student suddenly behaves in an uncharacteristic, disruptive manner, you need to find out why. A one-to-one problem-solving conference will give you the opportunity to hear the student out and to demonstrate that you care and are there to help.

- **Meet with a student in a one-to-one problem-solving conference when there is a serious problem.**

    Serious problems such as fighting cannot be overlooked. In addition to whatever consequence the student has received, you need to help redirect the student's anger.

Often when a teacher meets with a student under any of these these circumstances the meeting becomes a lecture from teacher to student, with the teacher overreacting to the student's behavior problems, doing all the talking and setting a punitive tone to the meeting. That is not the intent of this conference.

The Cue Card on page 110 gives guidelines for conducting a one-to-one problem-solving conference. Use the Problem-Solving Conference Worksheet that follows to plan and document problem-solving conferences you have with students.

CueCard

Conducting a One-to-One Problem-Solving Conference
Page 110

Problem-Solving Worksheet
Page 111

Cue Card

for _____

Defusing a Covert Confrontation

A **covert** confrontation occurs when a student responds to you with a sneer, a dirty look, mumbles under his or her breath or does something hostile that others in the class are unaware of.

Here's what to do in response to a covert confrontation:

First, calm yourself.

To stay in control you must decrease your anxiety and your body's natural inclination to react. *Above all, stay calm.* Count to three, four or five. Take a deep breath. Say to yourself, "Don't get angry. Don't get upset." Remind yourself not to take it personally.

Next, disengage from the student.

It's very natural to feel angry when a student sneers at you or gives you a dirty look. Your first reaction may be to lash back at the student: "Don't give me that look, young man," or "What did I hear you say?"

These responses are an invitation to the student to argue and get involved confrontationally.

Get some distance. Step away from the student. By putting distance between the two of you, you will give the student an opening to save face, back down and choose the appropriate behavior you need.

Remember, if the confrontation escalates, the student will be far less likely to choose appropriate behavior. *Keep your real goal in mind.*

If necessary, speak to the student later.

Covert behavior cannot necessarily be ignored. You have a responsibility to hold a student accountable for his or her behavior. Deal with it later, when the situation has cooled down. Let the student know that you will speak with him or her after class or after school.

N O T E S

_____
_____
_____
_____
_____
_____
_____
_____
_____
_____
_____
_____
_____
_____
_____
_____
_____
_____
_____

Cue Card

for _____

Defusing an Overt Confrontation

An **overt** confrontation occurs when a student blatantly comes after you and the whole class is aware of it. The student may verbally defy your authority, be insulting or talk back.

Here's what to do in response to an overt confrontation:

First, calm yourself.
Take a deep breath and tell yourself, "This student is very angry. He wants me to argue with him. I am not going to argue. I am going to stay calm. *It's not personal.*"

Next, use a paradoxical response.
To defuse an immediate situation, respond in the opposite way the student expects you to. If the student is shouting, speak softly. If the student yells even louder, speak more softly still. This technique will put the student off guard and help you deescalate the situation.

Why?

When you use a paradoxical response, you demonstrate that you are in control and are staying in control. You are not becoming part of an argument.

• When you do speak, refocus the conversation.
Put yourself inside the student's emotional turmoil and acknowledge his or her feelings. The feelings, after all, are real. Then calmly refocus the conversation back to what you need him or her to do.

"Lance, I can see that you don't want to join your group. I hear that you really don't want to do it. But it's your responsibility and you need to do it."

"It's clear to me that you really don't want to take this test today, Josh. I do hear you. But it's your job to take the test."

• If necessary, move the student away from peers.
If refocusing or a paradoxical response does not work, and the student continues to be confrontational, you may need to have the student move away from the rest of the class so you can speak to him or her privately. By removing the student from his or her audience, you lessen the likelihood of the student feeling compelled to act even tougher.

Once the student is moved away from the class, speak calmly and quietly and repeat what you want the student to do.

Note: For complete scripts, scenarios and guidelines for handling a wider variety of confrontational situations, please see Lee Canter's *Succeeding With Difficult Students.*

N O T E S
_____
_____
_____
_____
_____
_____
_____

STUDENT FILE COPY

DATE:

Cue Card

for _____

Conducting a One-to-One Problem-Solving Conference

Follow these guidelines when conducting a problem-solving conference:

Meet privately with the student.
Your conference should be confidential. Make sure there are no other students around to overhear or disrupt your meeting. The meeting should also be brief, a maximum of 10 to 15 minutes.

Show empathy and concern.
Focus on helping the student gain insight into his or her present behavior and understand why he or she needs to choose more responsible behavior. Be sure the student knows you are having the meeting because you care and want to help, not because you want to embarrass or punish.

Question the student to find out why there is a problem.
Listen to the student's point of view. Is there something happening at home, with other students or with a particular student that is upsetting? Is the work too hard?

Determine what you can do to help.
After listening to what the student has to say, you may discover there is a simple answer that will get him or her back on track. It's unlikely that the problem will be soved so easily, but it's worth considering.

Determine how the student can improve his or her behavior.
Focus part of your meeting on what the student can choose to do differently in the future that will enable him or her to handle the problem more effectively. Talk about the situation. Listen to the student's input. If need be, teach behaviors to the student.

State your own expectations about how the student is to behave.
In spite of the empathetic and caring attitude you are communicating, the student must clearly understand that you are very serious about not allowing misbehavior to continue. He or she must understand that under no circumstances will you allow the student to engage in disruptive behavior.

N O T E S

_____
_____
_____
_____
_____
_____
_____
_____
_____
_____
_____

STUDENT NAME:

CLASS/PERIOD:

Problem-Solving Conference
WORKSHEET

Student's name _____ Date _____

Reason for the conference:_____
_____
_____
_____
_____

Student input regarding the problem (Why does the student think this problem is occuring?) _____
_____
_____
_____
_____
_____

Steps the teacher can take to help solve the problem:_____
_____
_____
_____
_____
_____

Actions the student can take to solve the problem:_____
_____
_____
_____
_____
_____

State your expectations about how the student is to behave._____
_____
_____
_____
_____

Follow-up/Notes:_____
_____
_____
_____
_____

Student File Update

STUDENT FILE COPY

At this point your Student File should contain the following:

☑ Phone Call Record Sheet

☑ Relationship-Building Plan

☑ Student Interest Inventory

☑ 15+ Ways to Develop Positive Relationships with Students

☑ Primary Need Worksheet

☑ Goals Sheet

☑ Behavior Profile

☑ Lesson Plan(s) for Teaching Appropriate Behavior

☑ Providing Positive Support Cue Card

☑ Positive Phone Call Planner

☑ Redirecting Technique Cue Card

☑ Cue Card for Providing Consequences

☑ Cue Card for Defusing Covert Confrontations

☑ Cue Card for Defusing Overt Confrontations

☑ Cue Card for Conducting a Problem-Solving Conference

☑ Problem-Solving Conference Worksheet

☐ Any documentation pertaining to an Individualized Behavior Plan you are using with the student.

☐ Substitute's Plan

Reminders

- Difficult students are often masters at pushing the buttons that send teachers' tempers soaring. To avoid the reactive responses that are so detrimental to your relationship with a student, keep the following points in mind:

  – When a student becomes increasingly upset or defiant, you *can* stay calm and deescalate the situation.

  – When meeting in a problem-solving conference with a student you *can* communicate both firmness and caring.

- Effective communication skills will enable you to continue to build trust with a student even in difficult situations.

Your Next Step

Now is the time to evaluate your progress in working with your difficult student. See the "Where Are You Now?" page that follows.

Where are you now?

Take a moment to ask yourself the following questions:

- Are you building a positive relationship with your difficult student?

- Have you identified the student's primary need?

- Have you taught your student appropriate behavior for specific activities?

- Are you positively reinforcing the student when he or she chooses appropriate behavior?

- Are you redirecting nondisruptive off-task behavior?

- Are you using appropriate consequences consistently and fairly?

- Are you using communication skills to help ensure that all of your interactions with the student are directed toward building a trusting relationship?

If you can answer yes to all of these questions, and your student's behavior in one activity has improved, go back and teach behavior for another.

☆ Continue to reinforce appropriate behavior.

☆ Continue to use consequences when necessary.

☆ And above all, continue building your relationship with the student. Difficult students do not become difficult overnight. It's going to take consistent effort and commitment to succeed with these students.

If you can answer yes to all of these questions, and you are still having problems, you need to move to the next step. The following section, Additional Strategies, will introduce you to stronger, more individualized strategies—Individualized Behavior Plans.

Part 8

Additional Strategies

By applying the techniques and skills presented to this point, you will be able to help most of your difficult students make better choices, improve their behavior and sustain that improvement for long periods of time.

There will, however, still be some students whose behavior does not improve to a satisfactory level, or who are not able to sustain the improvements beyond a very short period of time.

With these students, the behavior management strategies you have tried so far will need to be augmented with additional, more individualized strategies.

How can you tell when you need to apply additional strategies in order to help your difficult student?

- If you have applied the techniques presented to this point and the student is still continually disruptive, off task, or is not completing assignments, you need to further individualize your efforts.

- If you have applied the techniques presented to this point and you find yourself giving more and more consequences, or the consequences that have been used are no longer effective, you need to further individualize your efforts.

- If you have applied the techniques presented to this point and you find yourself becoming more and more frustrated and angry with the student, you need to further individualize your efforts.

The best way to individualize further is to develop an Individualized Behavior Plan, or contract, for your student. An Individualized Behavior Plan is tightly structured and includes the following:

- Specific behaviors required of the student.

- More frequent motivation (positively reinforcement) for the student's appropriate behavior.

- Stronger, more meaningful consequences for inappropriate behavior.

- Specific relationship-building goals you will set for this student.

There are three types of Individualized Behavior Plans you can use:

Individualized Classroom Plan

Home-School Plan

Administrator Plan

Individualized Classroom Plan

A Classroom Plan gives you the opportunity to provide your student more structured intervention within your classroom.

The plan consists of the following:

1 **Specific behaviors** you expect of the student.

2 **Positive support** you will give the student for choosing appropriate behavior.

3 **Corrective action** you will take each time the student chooses inappropriate behavior.

4 **Relationship-building goals** you are committed to fulfilling.

Follow these steps:

STEP ONE: Select specific behaviors to focus on.

Use your student's Behavior Profile to select one or two (and only one or two) of his or her most disruptive or chronic behaviors.

STEP TWO: Develop a structured positive motivation system to help the student choose the appropriate behavior.

The positive motivation system must consist of the following:

• A specified reward the student will earn for appropriate behavior.

• The length of time you want the student to take to earn the reward.

• How you will track and acknowledge appropriate behavior.

For example:

Elementary

– For each 30 minutes that you do not shout and you keep your hands and feet to yourself, you will receive a check on a tracking chart. When all of the spaces on the chart are checked off, you will earn a lunch with the teacher.

Middle School/Secondary

– For each period during which you do not talk back or do not refuse to work, you will receive a point. When you earn five points you will receive a certificate you can use at the cafeteria.

STEP THREE: Select Consequences

Under the terms of an Individualized Behavior Plan, a consequence must be given every time the student chooses inappropriate behavior. No warnings. No second chances.

Therefore, select the consequence with care. Be sure it is one that you can and will deliver consistently, and one that will meet the student's specific need.

Students Who Need Attention

Consequences that work best with students who need attention are those that isolate them from their peers and the attention they want.

• Time out in another classroom

When a student is highly disruptive, it may be useful to send him or her to another classroom. There are several guidelines you must follow when using time out in another classroom:

- Send the student to a well-run classroom.

- The student should be sent to the same or a higher grade level. The student should not be sent to a lower grade level because it would be considered humiliating.

- The student should stay for a limited amount of time, do academic work and possibly fill out a Think Sheet (see page 99).

- When the time is up, the teacher should send the student back to your classroom.

This corrective action is highly effective with students who seek attention because they are removed from the peers whose attention they seek.

- Lunch detention

- After-school Detention

Students Who Need Limits

Confrontational students believe they can intimidate you and often act as though they do not care about any limits you set. Because they are in a power struggle with you, you need to provide the firmest limits possible.

- Tape record the student's behavior.

   Difficult students, particularly those who need limits, are often highly manipulative and will try to convince parents that you are picking on them—that they are doing nothing wrong. Recording their behavior is an extremely effective technique to use.

Here's how to use this consequence:

When a student disrupts, place a cassette recorder next to him or her and press "record." Tell the student that the recorder will remain on for the rest of the day or period and that you will play the recorded tape for his or her parents and/or the administrator. By turning on the tape recorder, you are sending a strong message to the student that you will follow through. Most often, this technique stops the inappropriate behavior immediately.

- Have the student call parents. (See pages 97-98.)

- Time out in another classroom (See pages 116-117.)

Students Who Need Motivation

Your goal with these students is for them to complete assigned work. For this reason, all consequences included in an Individualized Classroom Plan should be related to finishing the assignment.

- Incomplete work will be finished during after-school or lunch detention.

STEP FOUR: Set a relationship-building goal.

Commit yourself to specific actions that will help build your positive relationship with this student.

For example:

- Spend time problem-solving with the student on a one-to-one basis.

- Attend a sports event the student is involved in.

- Have lunch with the student.

- Bring books or other materials to the student that are of special interest.

- If appropriate, visit the student at his or her place of employment.

Use the Individualized Classroom Behavior Plan on page 123 to help you develop a Classroom Plan for your student.

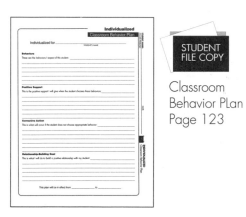

Classroom
Behavior Plan
Page 123

The Cue Card on page 124 gives you guidelines for introducing the Classroom Plan to your student.

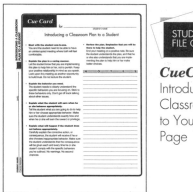

CueCard
Introducing a
Classroom Plan
to Your Student
Page 124

The Evaluation Sheet on page 125 will help you to determine what to do when the plan has been in effect for a specified period of time.

Classroom Plan
Evaluation
Page 125

Home-School Plan

Teachers sometimes find that a Home-School Plan that focuses on parental follow-through at home rather than teacher follow-through at school is an effective strategy to use with difficult students.

A Home-School Plan consists of the following:

1 **Specific behaviors** you expect of the student.

2 **Positive support** parents will give the student for choosing appropriate behavior at school.

3 **Corrective action** parents will take each time the student chooses inappropriate behavior at school.

4 **Relationship-building goals** you are committed to fulfilling.

A Home-School Plan is a collaborative effort between you and parents. Its success depends upon a parent's willingness to follow through consistently at home. It is important that you have a clear plan of action in mind before you meet with a parent.

Be prepared to discuss the following:

• **The specific behaviors you expect of the student.**

Tell the parent the exact behaviors you have observed the child engage in. Avoid value judgements such as "Your child has a bad attitude," or "She is always causing problems in class." Comments like these give no real information to the parent and can easily trigger defensive, angry responses. Be specific. Explain exactly how the student is noncompliant, and have documentation with you to use if necessary.

• **The steps you have already taken to help the student choose more appropriate behavior.**

The parent will want to know that you have already taken steps to help the student. Be sure to explain to the parent exactly what you have done to attempt to solve the problem on your own. Again, have documentation with you.

• **Suggest positives and consequences the parent can use at home.**

A parent may have no idea what constitutes an appropriate consequence or reward. Your suggestions can provide important guidance. Explain that the student does not always need to earn a "prize" each day, but rather can earn points toward a reward. Your suggestions should reflect the student's age and your own knowledge of the student's needs. Before the meeting ends, you will want to agree upon both the positive recognition and consequences the parent will provide each day.

Note: The "You Did It" coupons on page 131 can be given to parents to use as recognition for their child's good behavior. They will help parents structure their own positive reinforcement.

"You Did It"
Coupons
Page 131

- **The way you will communicate the student's behavior to the parent.**

Tell the parent that each day you will send a note home to let him or her know how the student behaved that day. A positive report means the student will receive the predetermined reward from the parent. A negative report means that the parent will provide the prearranged consequence.

Note: Use the Home-School Communication Forms (elementary, page 129 and secondary, page 130) to communicate with a parent about a student's behavior. Add comments of your own to these forms to keep the parents involved and confident. You may wish to keep a duplicate in your Student File.

Use the planning sheet on pages 126-127 to help you prepare for a parent conference to introduce a Home-School Plan.

Write your finished plan on the form on page 128. The Evaluation Sheet on page 132 will help you determine what to do when the plan has been in effect for a specified period of time.

Continue to build the positive relationship.

To further enhance the home-school partnership you are encouraging, set relationship-building goals that reach both student and parent.

For example:

- Positive phone calls to parent at home

- Positive phone calls to student

- Positive notes home

- If appropriate, a positive home visit

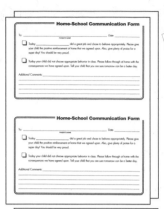

Home-School Communication Forms
Pages 129-130

Parent Conference Planning Sheet
Pages 126-127

Home-School Plan
Page 128

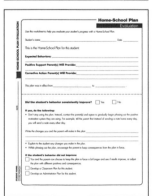

Home-School Plan Evaluation
Page 132

Administrator Plan

The involvement of your administrator (or other support staff) in an Individualized Behavior Plan can have a powerful impact on a student. Your administrator may not only be able to provide stronger, more effective consequences, but he or she can also provide unique motivation and help to develop a positive relationship with this student.

An Administrator Plan consists of the following:

1 **Specific behaviors** you expect of the student.

2. **Positive support** the administrator will give the student for choosing appropriate behavior.

3 **Corrective action** the administrator will take each time the student chooses inappropriate behavior.

4 **Relationship-building goals** that the administrator is committed to fulfilling.

How can administrator involvement benefit the needs of different students?

Students Who Need Attention

You know that these students want attention from you and from peers. But they may *really* be motivated to behave if they have an opportunity to receive special recognition from the principal. Rewards such as lunch with the principal, or a special certificate or personal note of congratulations can have great impact on a student who, above all, craves and needs attention.

Appropriate relationship-building activities an administrator might choose could be having lunch with a student (elementary) or going to an event in which the student is participating (middle/secondary).

Students Who Need Limits

What is often overlooked with power students is the fact that though they may not want attention or support from you, they may like the support or positive reinforcement they receive from the administrator or other support staff at school. ("I'm going to deal with the top guy!")

An Individualized Behavior Plan that includes recognition from an administrator may motivate this student where your own recognition did not.

Likewise, firmer corrective actions such as in-school suspension and conferencing with parents can also be provided through the administrator.

Appropriate relationship-building activities an administrator might choose could be coming to class each day and spending five minutes helping the student (elementary) or meeting one-to-one with the student on a regular basis (middle/secondary).

Students Who Need Motivation

There are some unmotivated students who just will not work for you. But they may be motivated by the recognition and reinforcement of the administrator or other support staff at school. One effective way to involve the administrator is to ask him or her to help the student get started on assignments.

The administrator can also be involved in holding the student accountable for completing work. Some administrators have students stay in their office after school to complete assignments, or just show them the completed work. Others establish study halls where students need to go to complete work they have not completed in class. These special study halls are monitored closely by an adult, and students are expected to complete their work there.

Appropriate relationship-building activities an administrator might choose could be spending time with the student.

Use the reproducible Administrator Plan on page 133 to help you and your administrator develop an individualized plan for your student.

The Evaluation Sheet on page 134 will help you determine what to do when the plan has been in effect for a specified period of time.

Reproducible positive notes from an administrator to student can be found on pages 135-136. Pass these along to your administrator for use with your student.

Administrator
Plan
Page 133

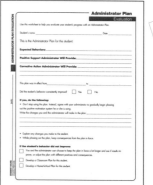

Administrator
Plan
Evaluation
Page 134

Positive
Notes
Elementary
Page 135

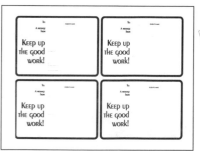

Positive
Notes
Middle School/
Secondary
Page 136

Individualized
Classroom Behavior Plan

Individualized for _____
STUDENT'S NAME

Behaviors

These are the behaviors I expect of this student: _____

_____

_____

_____

_____

_____

Positive Support

This is the positive support I will give when the student chooses these behaviors: _____

_____

_____

_____

_____

_____

Corrective Action

This is what will occur if the student does not choose appropriate behavior: _____

_____

_____

_____

_____

_____

Relationship-Building Goal

This is what I will do to build a positive relationship with my student: _____

_____

_____

_____

_____

This plan will be in effect from _____ to _____ .

STUDENT FILE COPY

DATE:

Cue Card

for _____

Introducing a Classroom Plan to a Student

- **Meet with the student one-to-one.**
  You and the student need to be able to have an uninterrupted meeting where both will feel comfortable.

- **Explain the plan in a caring manner.**
  Let the student know that you are implementing this plan to help him or her, not to punish. Keep your positive relationship in mind as you speak. Look upon this meeting as another opportunity to build trust. Do not lecture the student.

- **Explain the behavior you need.**
  The student needs to clearly understand the specific behaviors you are focusing on. Stick to these behaviors only. Don't get off track talking about other issues.

- **Explain what the student will earn when he or she behaves appropriately.**
  Tell the student what you are going to do to help him or her choose appropriate behavior. Make sure the student understands exactly how and when he or she will earn the reward or privilege.

- **Explain what will happen if the student does not behave appropriately.**
  Carefully explain the corrective action, or consequence, the student will receive if he or she chooses inappropriate behavior. Make sure the student understands that the consequence will be given each and every time he or she doesn't comply with the specific behaviors you've outlined. No warnings. No second chances.

- **Review the plan. Emphasize that you will be there to help the student.**
  End your meeting on a positive note. Be sure the student understands the plan, and that he or she also understands that you are implementing the plan to help him or her make better choices.

N O T E S

_____
_____
_____
_____
_____
_____
_____
_____
_____
_____
_____
_____
_____
_____
_____
_____
_____
_____
_____
_____
_____
_____
_____

Classroom Plan
Evaluation

Use this worksheet to help you evaluate your student's progress with a Classroom Plan.

Student's name _____ Date _____

This is the Individualized Classroom Plan for this student:

Behaviors: _____

_____

Positive Support: _____

_____

Corrective Action: _____

_____

This plan was in effect from _____ to _____.

- -

Did the student's behavior consistently improve? ☐ Yes   ☐ No

If yes, do the following:

• Don't stop using the plan. Instead, gradually begin phasing out the positive motivation system you are using by decreasing the number of positives earned in a specific time period or increasing the time needed to earn the reward.

Write the changes you will make in the plan: _____

_____

_____

• Explain to the student any changes you make in the plan.

• While phasing out the plan, keep consequences from the plan in force.

If the student's behavior did not improve:

☐ You can choose to keep the plan in force a bit longer and see if results improve, or adjust the positives or consequences in the plan.

☐ Develop a Home-School Plan for this student.

☐ Develop an Administrator Plan for this student.

© 1993 Lee Canter & Associates

STUDENT
FILE COPY

Use this sheet to plan your conference.

Student's name _____ Date _____

Begin with a statement of concern. _____
_____
_____
_____
_____
_____

Describe the specific inappropriate behavior the student engages in. _____
_____
_____
_____
_____
_____
_____
_____

Tell the parent the steps you have already taken to handle the problem. _____
_____
_____
_____
_____
_____
_____
_____

Ask for parental input. (Write response notes here.) _____
_____
_____
_____
_____
_____
_____
_____

STUDENT NAME:

CLASS/PERIOD:

DATE:

Let the parent know that you have a plan of action in mind. Emphasize that you cannot do it on your own—that you must have parental help. _____

_____

_____

_____

_____

_____

Introduce the concept of a Home-School Plan and together agree upon the actions the parent will take at home in response to the student's behavior. _____

_____

_____

_____

_____

_____

_____

_____

Tell the parent that you will send home a note each day. _____

_____

_____

_____

_____

_____

_____

_____

Explain the Home-School Plan to the student (if appropriate, the student can be asked to join the meeting at this point). _____

_____

_____

_____

_____

_____

_____

_____

_____

Notes _____

_____

_____

PARENT CONFERENCE for a Home-School Plan SIDE 2

Home-School Plan

STUDENT FILE COPY

DATE:

STUDENT NAME:

CLASS/PERIOD:

For _____
STUDENT'S NAME

Behaviors

These are the behaviors I expect of this student: _____
_____
_____
_____
_____

Communication with Parents

This is how the parent(s) will be informed of the student's behavior each day: _____
_____
_____
_____
_____

Positive Support

This is the positive support the parent(s) will give when the student chooses these behaviors: _____
_____
_____
_____
_____

Corrective Action

This is the corrective action the parent(s) will provide if the student does not choose appropriate behavior:
_____
_____
_____
_____

Relationship-Building Goal

This is what I will do to continue to build a positive relationship with this student: _____
_____
_____
_____
_____

This plan will be in effect from _____ to_____.

Home-School Communication Form

To: _____ Date _____

PARENT'S NAME

☐ Today _____ did a great job and chose to behave appropriately. Please give your child the positive reinforcement at home that we agreed upon. Also, give plenty of praise for a super day! You should be very proud.

☐ Today your child did not choose appropriate behavior in class. Please follow through at home with the consequences we have agreed upon. Tell your child that you are sure tomorrow can be a better day.

Additional Comments: _____
_____
_____
_____
_____

Home-School Communication Form

To: _____ Date _____

PARENT'S NAME

☐ Today _____ did a great job and chose to behave appropriately. Please give your child the positive reinforcement at home that we agreed upon. Also, give plenty of praise for a super day! You should be very proud.

☐ Today your child did not choose appropriate behavior in class. Please follow through at home with the consequences we have agreed upon. Tell your child that you are sure tomorrow can be a better day.

Additional Comments: _____
_____
_____
_____
_____

Home-School Communication Form

To: _____ Date _____
 PARENT'S NAME

From: _____ Class/Period _____

☐ Today your child chose appropriate behavior in class. Please follow through at home with the positive reinforcement we have agreed upon. Give your child plenty of praise for a job well done.

☐ Today your child did not choose appropriate behavior in class. Please follow through at home with the consequences we have agreed upon.

Additional Comments: _____
_____
_____
_____

Home-School Communication Form

To: _____ Date _____
 PARENT'S NAME

From: _____ Class/Period _____

☐ Today your child chose appropriate behavior in class. Please follow through at home with the positive reinforcement we have agreed upon. Give your child plenty of praise for a job well done.

☐ Today your child did not choose appropriate behavior in class. Please follow through at home with the consequences we have agreed upon.

Additional Comments: _____
_____
_____
_____

You did it and I'm proud of you!

In recognition of your good behavior,

you may stay up _____ minutes

later on _____ night.

You did it and I'm proud of you!

In recognition of your good behavior,

you may stay up _____ minutes

later on _____ night.

You did it and I'm proud of you!

In recognition of your improved behavior,

you may select the dinner menu

for _____ evening.

You did it and I'm proud of you!

In recognition of your improved behavior,

you may select the dinner menu

for _____ evening.

You did it and I'm proud of you!

In recognition of your improved behavior,

you may watch a television program

of your choice on _____ .

You did it and I'm proud of you!

In recognition of your improved behavior,

you may watch a television program

of your choice on _____ .

You did it and I'm proud of you!

In recognition of your improved behavior,

_____

_____ .

You did it and I'm proud of you!

In recognition of your improved behavior,

_____

_____ .

Home-School Plan
Evaluation

Use this worksheet to help you evaluate your student's progress with a Home-School Plan.

Student's name _____ Date _____

This is the Home-School Plan for this student:

Expected Behaviors: _____
_____

Positive Support Parent(s) Will Provide: _____
_____

Corrective Action Parent(s) Will Provide: _____
_____

This plan was in effect from _____ to _____ .

- -

Did the student's behavior consistently improve? ☐ Yes   ☐ No

If yes, do the following:

• Don't stop using the plan. Instead, contact the parent(s) and agree to gradually begin phasing out the positive motivation system they are using. For example, tell the parent that instead of sending a note home every day, you will send a note every other day.

Write the changes you and the parent will make in the plan: _____
_____
_____

• Explain to the student any changes you make in the plan.
• While phasing out the plan, encourage the parent to keep consequences from the plan in force.

If the student's behavior did not improve:

☐ You and the parent can choose to keep the plan in force a bit longer and see if results improve, or adjust the plan with different positives and consequences.

☐ Develop a Classroom Plan for this student.

☐ Develop an Administrator Plan for this student.

Administrator Plan

For _____
STUDENT'S NAME

Behaviors

These are the behaviors I expect of this student: _____

_____

_____

_____

Positive Support

This is the positive support the administrator will give when the student chooses these behaviors:

_____

_____

_____

Corrective Action

This is the corrective action the administrator will provide if the student does not choose appropriate behavior:

_____

_____

_____

Relationship-Building Goal

This is what the administrator will do to continue to build a positive relationship with this student:

_____

_____

_____

This plan will be in effect from _____ to _____ .

Notes

_____

_____

_____

_____

_____

_____

Administrator Plan
Evaluation

Use this worksheet to help you evaluate your student's progress with an Administrator Plan.

Student's name _____ Date _____

This is the Administrator Plan for this student:

Expected Behaviors: _____
_____

Positive Support Administrator Will Provide: _____
_____

Corrective Action Administrator Will Provide: _____
_____
_____

This plan was in effect from _____ to _____

Did the student's behavior consistently improve? ☐ Yes ☐ No

If yes, do the following:

• Don't stop using the plan. Instead, agree with your administrator to gradually begin phasing out the positive motivation system he or she is using.

Write the changes you and the administrator will make in the plan: _____
_____
_____
_____

• Explain any changes you make to the student.
• While phasing out the plan, keep consequences from the plan in force.

If the student's behavior did not improve:

☐ You and the administrator can choose to keep the plan in force a bit longer and see if results improve, or adjust the plan with different positives and consequences.

☐ Develop a Classroom Plan for this student.

☐ Develop a Home-School Plan for this student.

A SPECIAL MESSAGE FROM THE PRINCIPAL

★ GREAT JOB
COMPLETING
YOUR
ASSIGNMENTS!

_____
STUDENT'S NAME

_____

_____

_____

_____

_____
PRINCIPAL'S SIGNATURE   DATE

A Special Message
from the Principal for _____
STUDENT'S NAME

_____

_____

_____

_____

 *You're doing a great job!*

_____
PRINCIPAL'S SIGNATURE   DATE

STUDENT'S NAME

To:

A MESSAGE FROM

KEEP UP THE GOOD WORK!

STUDENT'S NAME

To:

A MESSAGE FROM

KEEP UP THE GOOD WORK!

STUDENT'S NAME

To:

A MESSAGE FROM

KEEP UP THE GOOD WORK!

STUDENT'S NAME

To:

A MESSAGE FROM

KEEP UP THE GOOD WORK!

Student File Update

STUDENT FILE COPY

At this point your Student File should contain the following:

✓ Phone Call Record Sheet

✓ Relationship-Building Plan

✓ Student Interest Inventory

✓ 15+ Ways to Develop Positive Relationships with Students

✓ Primary Need Worksheet

✓ Goals Sheet

✓ Behavior Profile

✓ Lesson Plan(s) for Teaching Appropriate Behavior

✓ Providing Positive Support Cue Card

✓ Positive Phone Call Planner

✓ Redirecting Technique Cue Card

✓ Cue Card for Providing Consequences

✓ Cue Card for Defusing Covert Confrontations

✓ Cue Card for Defusing Overt Confrontations

✓ Cue Card for Conducting a Problem-Solving Conference

✓ Problem-Solving Conference Worksheet

✓ Any documentation pertaining to an Individualized Behavior Plan you are using with the student.

☐ Substitute's Plan

Reminders

• When you are working with students who require an Individualized Behavior Plan, there are often no simple answers. Some individualized plans may work for awhile. Then, in spite of everything you've done, you might find the student falling back into disruptive behavior patterns.

• With difficult students you need to be willing to consistently evaluate, restructure, and follow through on your behavior management efforts. Most of all, however, you must continue to build a positive relationship with the student.

What's Next?

Working with a difficult student is like riding a roller coaster. There will be ups, and, just as surely, there will be downs. You will need to respond to these ups and downs by evaluating, reassessing and trying different approaches as needed. Succeeding with difficult students takes perseverance and patience. And it takes a willingness to consistently communicate to the student that you aren't going away. This is a message that many students have never heard before.

When a difficult student realizes that a caring adult has made such a significant commitment, he or she may work to begin changing behavior and you will find yourself succeeding with difficult students.

Part 9

When you can't be there...

Your difficult student needs consistency. He or she needs to know that your expectations remain constant whether you are in the classroom or not.

It is very important, therefore, when you are out of the classroom, to give your substitute guidance in working with this student.

The Substitute's Plans on pages 140-142 will let your sub know exactly what you expect of your student, how he or she should respond to the student's appropriate behavior and what responses should be to inappropriate behavior.

Separate reproducible plans are provided for students who need attention, students who need firmer limits and students who need motivation. Each plan has been formatted with adequate open-ended space to allow you to give individualized information that will ensure a better day for both sub and student.

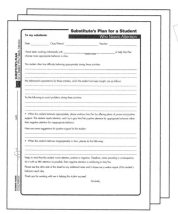

Substitute's Plan for a Student Who Needs
Attention, Page 140
Firmer Limits, Page 141
Motivation, Page 142

Fill out a form for each difficult student and keep it in your Student File, ready to use. Update as needed.

And when you return...

Substitute Thank-You

When you return to class and find that your sub has taken the time and made the effort to follow through with behavior management efforts on behalf of this student, let him or her know that you appreciate it.

Thank-you
Note
Page 143

Use the reproducible thank-you note on page 143, or write your own, using the "fold-a-note" on page 144.

Either way, this is a great way to both thank a fellow professional and spread the word that succeeding with a difficult student takes a concerted effort by all the adults in a student's life.

SUBSTITUTE'S PLAN
for a Student Who Needs Attention

STUDENT FILE COPY

To my substitute:

Date: _____ Class/Period: _____ Teacher: _____

I have been working individually with _____ to help him/her

STUDENT'S NAME

choose more appropriate behavior in class.

This student often has difficulty behaving appropriately during these activities:

_____

_____

_____

My behavioral expectations for these activities, which the student has been taught, are as follows:

_____

_____

_____

Try the following to avoid problems during these activities:

_____

_____

_____

• When this student behaves appropriately, please reinforce him/her by offering plenty of praise and positive support. This student needs attention, and I try to give him/her positive attention for *appropriate* behavior rather than negative attention for inappropriate behavior.

Here are some suggestions for positive support for this student:

_____

_____

• When this student behaves inappropriately in class, please do the following:

_____

_____

_____

Keep in mind that this student wants attention, positive *or* negative. Therefore, when providing a consequence, do it with as little attention as possible. Even negative attention is reinforcing to him/her.

Please see the other side of this sheet for any additional notes and to leave me a written report of this student's behavior each day.

Thank you for working with me in helping this student succeed.

Sincerely,

STUDENT NAME:

CLASS/PERIOD:

DATE:

Substitute's Plan for a Student
Who Needs Firmer Limits

To my substitute:

Date: _____ Class/Period: _____ Teacher: _____

I have been working individually with _____ to help him/her
                                                    STUDENT'S NAME
choose more appropriate behavior in class.

This student often has difficulty behaving appropriately during these activities:

_____

_____

My behavioral expectations for these activities, which the student has been taught, are as follows:

_____

_____

_____

Try the following to avoid problems during these activities:

_____

_____

_____

• When this student behaves appropriately, reinforce him/her in a very low key manner. This student will
not appreciate or respond well to "public" positive reinforcement.

Here are some suggestions for positive support for this student:

_____

_____

_____

• When this student behaves inappropriately, please do the following:

_____

_____

_____

Keep in mind that this student may be confrontational, especially when given a consequence. It is important,
therefore, to provide consequences in a very calm, quiet—but firm—manner.

Please see the other side of this sheet for any additional notes and to leave me a written report of this
student's behavior each day.

Thank you for working with me to help this student succeed.

                                                            Sincerely,

STUDENT FILE COPY

Substitute's Plan for a Student
Who Needs Motivation

To my substitute:

Date: _____ Class/Period: _____ Teacher: _____

I have been working individually with_____to help him/her

STUDENT'S NAME

complete assigned work in class.

Here are some suggestions that will help this student begin assignments and finish them:

_____

_____

_____

_____

_____

• When this student completes work, please tie your reinforcement to his/her academic effort. This student
needs constant encouragement. Provide reinforcement immediately, and in an individual and quiet manner.

Here are some suggestions for positive support for this student:

_____

_____

_____

_____

_____

_____

• If, however, this student does not complete classwork, please do the following:

_____

_____

_____

_____

_____

_____

Please see the other side of this sheet for any additional notes and to leave me a written report of this student's
behavior each day. Thank you for working with me in helping this student succeed.

Sincerely,

Dear

Thank you for the care and attention you gave to working with_____ in my class.

This student's success is very important to all of us at school, and I want you to know how much I appreciate the fact that you became part of our efforts to build that success.

When a student knows that adults in his or her life are dedicated to his well being, self-esteem rises and so does achievement.

Thank you for being in my class and making a difference with this student.

Sincerely,

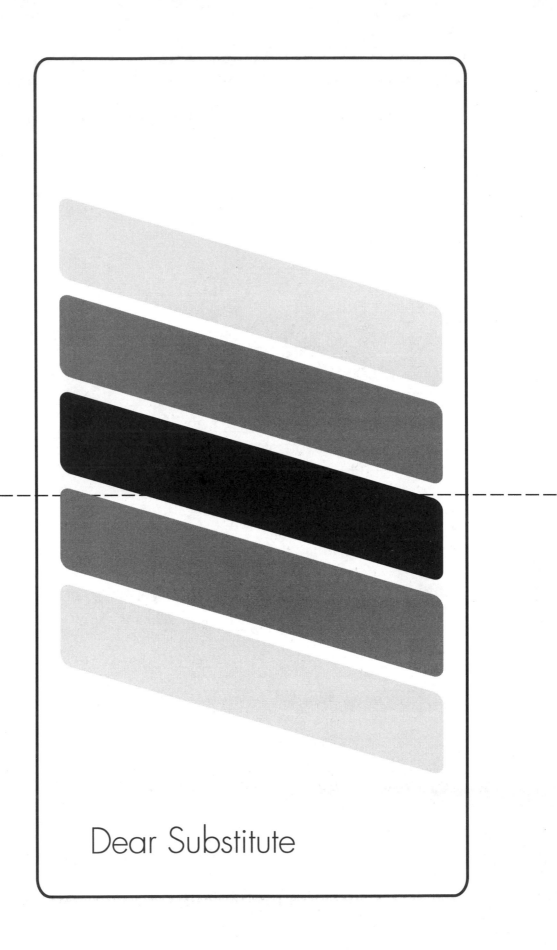

Dear Substitute